GOD ON THE MOVE

God on the Move

*"A whistle-stop tour of the Christian mission today . . .
In a day when we need to be both global citizens and
Christian disciples, he gives us an up-to-date glimpse
into how God's kingdom of righteousness, peace and joy
is doing in the world."*
Rt. Rev. Patrick B. Harris, Bishop of Southwell.

*"Martin is well qualified to give an optimistic, realistic
and challenging overview of the world mission scene . . .
He challenges us all not to remain in blinkered
insularity from the real world."*
David Evans, General Secretary, South American
Mission Society.

*"Martin Goldsmith challenges the poverty of vision
many of us are content to tolerate. Little wonder
contentment with the status quo prevails in so many of
churches . . . Read this book and be given a holy
discontent with the way things are, and allow the spirit
of God to give you fresh motivation to give your life to
the Lord Jesus Christ for the greatest task in the world.*
John Wallis, EMA Consultant and former Director
of OMF International.

GOD ON THE MOVE

Growth and Change in the Church Worldwide

By
Martin Goldsmith

OM
publishing

Copyright © 1991 Martin Goldsmith

First published in 1991 by MARC,
an imprint of Monarch Publications Ltd.,
Eastbourne, E Sussex

This edition published in 1998 by OM Publishing
04 03 02 01 00 99 98   7 6 5 4 3 2 1

OM Publishing is an imprint of Paternoster Publishing,
P.O. Box 300, Carlisle, Cumbria, CA3 0QS, U.K.
http://www.paternoster-publishing.com

The right of Martin Goldsmith to be identified as the Author of
this Work has been asserted by him in accordance with the
Copyright, Design and Patents Act 1988.

British Library Cataloguing in Publication Data

A catalogue record for this book is available from
the British Library.

ISBN 1-85078-304-7

Cover Design by Mainstream, Lancaster
Typeset by WestKey Ltd., Falmouth, Cornwall
Printed in Great Britain by
Caledonian International Book Manufacturing Ltd, Glasgow

Contents

1

It's God's world and God works in it

God never stands still

When I was a young theological student back in the 1950s, we were all challenged to pray fervently for mission to Latin America. As we shall note in chapter 5, Latin America presented evangelical witness with a tough and unyielding front. Struggling little churches faced fierce opposition and persecution from an unreformed and corrupt Roman Catholicism. Many of my contemporaries went as missionaries in response to this challenge.

When God stirs his church to fervent prayer and to active mission, there can be little doubt that God is planning to work in a new and exciting way. So it was in Latin America. The Holy Spirit called people to pray and to go in mission – and then he broke into the whole situation in a way that has changed the whole continent.

Some years later God changed direction and began to challenge his people all over the world to pray for persecuted Christians in the Communist world. Many Christians followed in the footsteps of Brother Andrew in taking Bibles into those countries. Support and fellowship flowed through the iron and bamboo curtains to those churches which were facing such fearfully difficult days. God called his people to pray and to be active in mission – and then again God stepped in and we have seen the miracle of God's working in those lands.

Now God is calling his people in every continent to pray and work in mission for the Muslim world. I am excited to see in country after country how Christians are experiencing a new passion for witness to Muslims. Surely God has plans for our Muslim friends in the coming years.

God moves on. He never stands still. In the first centuries Israel and the Middle East were the great centre of the Christian faith. But God moved on along the shores of North Africa and southern Europe until those areas became the heartlands of the church. To everyone's surprise the centre of the Christian faith moved north and the formerly primitive tribes of central and northern Europe took on the responsibility of representing Christ in the world. Their migrations carried the gospel to the dynamic new territories of North America and Australasia. And their missionaries ventured into Africa, Asia and the rest of the world.

Now in our day we are sometimes surprised to discover that such 'mission field' countries have overtaken the West. It is their churches which show enormous growth and lead us all in their example of dynamic and confident witness, deep spirituality and prayer.

No longer can we divide the world into those countries which send missionaries and those which need their evangelistic witness. Almost everywhere in the world the church of Jesus Christ is to be found – and yet all of us also still need the input of missionaries from other countries, cultures and churches. But western Christians need constantly to be reminded that today some 60 per cent of the world's Christians live in the southern hemisphere.

The global village

Times have changed remarkably in the years since my wife and I enjoyed three weeks on a liner en route to Singapore as new missionaries. Asia seemed then a very long way away, and most people knew little about such distant parts of the world.

In 1960 television was still an unusual addition to the home, so few people had seen live pictures of remote countries. Air travel was expensive, and long sea journeys were required if you needed to visit other continents.

Today things are very different. Television has brought the whole world into our sitting rooms and relatively cheap air travel has opened the door for multitudes to visit other countries. Not only do missionaries, business people and diplomats enjoy this opportunity, but the travel agents beckon the tourist to adventurous holidays in all parts of the world. Many Europeans have had holidays in the Muslim countries of North Africa or Turkey. A few have ventured into very different cultural situations in

Nepal, India or even remote tribal areas. The exotic beauties of Thailand, Malaysia, Indonesia or Japan are no longer tied to the missionaries' slide shows, but have become the living experience of many.

No longer can we afford to remain in blinkered insularity. What happens in one part of the world affects us all. Political changes in Eastern Europe influence our political and economic climate. Marxist communism has been fearfully discredited – how will that affect the thinking of our university and college lecturers? Will it change the whole philosophical and religious approach in Western Europe? Tensions in the Middle East and the Gulf affect race relations in Britain as Muslims voice their disillusionment with our government's policies and feel that the crusading spirit of imperialism threatens the Muslim world again. Our stock market and economy shiver at every uncertainty on the world scene. No country or people today can live in isolation like ostriches with their heads in the sand – we all depend on each other.

So the Christian needs to understand what is happening in the world of our day.

God's world

The Bible never lets us forget that God created the world, everything in it and all people of every race and background. Again and again the Bible reminds us that God is not some irrelevant old gentleman sitting impotently in heaven while things on earth develop independently of him. From the Bible it is clear that he is the sovereign Lord who controls the movements of history with his own purposes in mind. He not only controls those who believe in him and desire to follow his will, but also has the power to use men like Pharaoh, Nebuchadnezzar and Cyrus as his instruments. The rise and fall of empires is in his hands.

What are his purposes in history? What should we be looking for, and thinking of, as we read our newspaper, watch our television and pray about the world?

In Colossians 1:16 we read that everything was created by the Lord and for him. The fundamental purpose of this world is to give him pleasure. And what an amazing privilege it is that mere human beings like us can by our faith and godly holiness bring a smile onto the face of almighty God! As Christians we long that the people of all nations would so honour Jesus Christ that they would live for his glory and pleasure. At present many seem to live for the satisfaction of their own selfish desires and to bolster their pride – this is true of nation states as well as individual human beings. What a difference it would make if everybody and every society or nation made it their aim to please the Lord.

What does it mean in practice to live for God's pleasure?

The Bible talks much about God's kingdom as his purpose and our goal. In Romans 14:17 Paul lists three fundamental characteristics of God's kingdom. Righteousness, peace and joy in the Holy Spirit are what God looks for in this world and what we should work and pray for. Paul goes on to declare that these characteristics are the true marks of serving Christ. Without Jesus Christ it will prove impossible to develop lives and societies where purity, holiness and godly righteousness reign. Peace too will elude us. Broken or strained relationships, racial tensions, class divisions, generation gaps, international selfishness and even warfare – all these tragic realities will be only too common if Jesus Christ is not acknowledged as King. Without the Holy Spirit there can be no deep, constant joy in life.

Evangelism is therefore essential to help people to honour and please the Lord. But God does not only look for people to come to faith in Christ for their own salvation. We are also called to serve the Lord in personal and social righteousness, in peace and peaceful relationships, with an infectious joy in the Holy Spirit.

In this book we want to look at what God is doing in the various parts of the world today. We shall want to see whether people are coming to faith in Christ and thus beginning to live for his pleasure and glory. We shall want therefore also to see whether his church is growing numerically. But we shall have in mind the further question of whether these three marks of the presence of God's kingdom are in evidence.

Worldwide vision

There is always a danger that Christians become so preoccupied with their own country and people that they fail to gain an active interest in the rest of the world, or even in other races within their own country.

Such a narrow vision loses sight of God's deep concern for the whole world. God's great desire is that all peoples should come to faith in Jesus Christ and so enjoy the resurrection life in oneness with God the Father and with each other.

Narrow insularity is no new problem. The Jews in the Old Testament needed to be frequently reminded that the God of Israel was also the Lord of all the earth. And the New Testament shows us in Acts 10 how Peter needed a stomach-churning vision to make him willing to welcome gentiles. Paul too had to be pushed out into wider gentile mission beyond his own Jewish people. When the Jews of Antioch in Pisidia violently opposed the gospel and the gentiles eagerly accepted it, only then did Paul declare 'we turn to the gentiles'. The New Testament church faced the same pressing challenge. Should gentiles be evangelized and accepted into the church or was the Christian gospel fundamentally only for Jews and proselytes? Christians knew that God had created the world, not just Israel, but still they thought of him primarily as the God of Israel. They knew in theory that the kingdom of the Messiah was to be for all peoples, but they looked for a Messiah who would save his own people Israel. Much of the New Testament is written therefore to show that the good news of Jesus Christ is indeed for all peoples, and that Christians should share the gospel with all – Jews and gentiles of all races everywhere.

As the apostle to the gentiles, Paul is particularly keen to show that his calling is a valid one. For example, in Romans he argues that people of all races, Jews and gentiles alike, are under the power of

sin (Rom. 1:1–3, 20). He then shows that God has
provided a universally available solution to this uni-
versal problem of sin (3:21–26). The answer is in the
death of Jesus for our sins, the benefit of which we
receive through faith in Christ rather than through
following the commands of the Jewish law in the
covenant with Moses (e.g. Rom. 3:28). Faith in Christ
can be exercised by all peoples, not just by Jews. If
the Jewish law had been the means of salvation, then
the church would have remained exclusively for
Jews and those gentiles who joined themselves to the
people of Israel as proselytes. That is why Paul continues his argument by asking, 'or is God the God of
Jews only? Is he not the God of Gentiles also?' (Rom.
3:29). God has provided the way of redemption for
all peoples in Jesus Christ and it is our task to share
that good news throughout the world.

As Paul's companion in part of his missionary
journeys, Luke shares that same international vision.
We see this particularly clearly in his Acts of the
Apostles. Luke's thesis is that the Holy Spirit's power
sends Christ's disciples out as witnesses not only
among Jews in Jerusalem and Judea, but also among
the half-Jewish half-gentile Samaritans and then
among gentiles 'to the end of the earth' (Acts 1:8).
This is clear from the structure of the book.

The first seven chapters show the church's witness
among Jews and proselytes only. Then in Acts 8 we
are given two bridges to span the fearful gulf
between the Jews and the gentiles. Through persecution God pushed the young Jewish Christians to
widen their horizons. Philip evangelizes the Samaritans and is also led by the Spirit to bring the Ethiopian

eunuch to faith in Jesus as Messiah. The eunuch was almost certainly an African gentile, but we know he was already closely related to Israel in that he was going to worship in the Jerusalem temple and was reading the Hebrew Scriptures. Only after these two half-way houses between Jews and gentiles does Luke tell the story of the conversion of Paul, the apostle to the gentiles. In Acts 10 and 11 we read of the gentile Cornelius coming to faith in Jesus Christ. But still they 'spoke the word to none except Jews' (Acts 11:19), although the next verse shows that some ventured to preach also to Greeks. Finally in Acts 13 God reiterates the call to gentile mission which he gave Paul at his conversion. Because of the opposition which Paul and Barnabas encountered from the Jews they eventually made that crucial decision to turn to the gentiles. From then on the expansion of the church among the gentiles began to unfold alongside the ongoing evangelization of the Jews. And the church has continued to widen and grow throughout these past two thousand years. We today inherit that history and take our place in God's purposes for the preaching of the gospel to all peoples everywhere, to Jews and to gentiles.

Dark clouds and silver linings

When we examine the development of the church worldwide through the centuries and look at what God is doing in our generation, it is easy to be unbalanced. Some of us are natural optimists and enthusiasts, so are tempted to take note of the growth of the church and revival movements. But we may fail to take seriously the areas of defeat or stagnation. Others of us tend towards pessimism, so may concentrate on the fearful failures of the church and the overwhelming needs everywhere. Some of us believe that every small grey cloud is surrounded by wonderful silver linings, while others note that depressingly heavy grey clouds overshadow the sadly small silver linings.

We see this tension in the biblical teaching of the kingdom of God. Jesus announced that the kingdom had come and was now present among us. In the person of Jesus Christ the kingdom is already here. And yet he also taught his disciples to pray 'thy kingdom come' because the fullness of the kingdom is still a future hope which we pray and work for. The kingdom starts very small, grows and finally will be brought to its complete glory. Even Jesus himself, the King of the kingdom, came as a tiny baby, grew 'in wisdom and in stature, and in favour with God and man' (Lk. 2:52). Only then in his humanity did he ascend to assume again the fulness of his glory in the presence of his Father. The New Testament church also started very small. It began with a tiny handful of insignificant, unknown men and a few women. But it grew. The Book of Acts records how more and more believers were added to the church. And it spread from its purely Jewish base to reach out to the neighbouring gentile peoples of South Europe, North Africa and the Middle East. Then it gradually widened its outreach to India, China and North Europe. Today the church is to be found in every continent, although not yet in every race or every geographical area. The church still needs to expand.

Each individual Christian also starts the Christian life in weakness – the New Testament picture is of our being born again. We are always born small! Next the Christian should grow in grace, holiness and knowledge of the Lord. Finally we shall be perfectly holy as the Lord himself is holy; we shall love him fully; we shall know him perfectly.

God has already done great things, but there remains much which he has not yet done in each of us personally, in the church and in the world which he created and longs to bring to perfect redemption.

This combination of 'already' and 'not yet' in the work and life of God's kingdom leaves us with a certain tension. It is good to rejoice in all that God has already done for us, for our church, for the church worldwide and for the world. But if we forget our failure to achieve the fulness of God's glory, then we can easily become proudly triumphalistic and smug. We need to be deeply aware of our need for God to work more fully. But if we forget to be thankful for what God has already done, then we can become negatively critical, depressed and ungrateful.

When we read the mission reports of some Christians today, we get a glorious sense of revival breaking out everywhere and the church triumphant by God's Spirit. While it is true that our God is wonderfully at work, there also remain areas of the world where it is difficult to rejoice so confidently and in every part of the world there remains a considerable 'not yet' in the working of God's kingdom.

On the other hand there are other Christians

whose mission reports underline the overwhelming
need of unevangelized multitudes and the shocking
weaknesses of the church spiritually, morally and
socially. This apparent realism sometimes fails to
give God the glory for the great things he has already
done in and through his people. Realism should not
only be negative.

In this book I am very aware that I am writing
largely from my own perspective and experience, but
I will try to be truthful and not propagandist. I believe that our Lord Jesus is the truth (Jn 14:6) and
therefore it is vitally important for the Christian to be
like our Lord and Master. Like him we should be
careful that our words are true. Biased or one-sided
reporting will not convey 'the truth, the whole truth
and nothing but the truth'. We believe that our God
is perfect in what he does and in his timing. There is
no need either to embroider our reports of what he
has already wonderfully done, or emphasize unduly
what he has not yet done. We can trust him to do his
work in his own perfect time and way.

Throughout this book many statistics will be
quoted and I am indebted to P. Johnstone's *Operation
World* and other books, but it should be noted that all
mission statistics remain somewhat unreliable. For
example, I was recently sent a list of so-called 'unreached peoples'. In each case where the statistics
related to a country we knew personally we found
them gravely inaccurate. One somewhat amusing
statistic was that there is only one Christian among
British Jews – some of my Jewish Christian friends
and I have wondered which of us it is! For this reason
I shall not follow the pattern of many who write and

speak about mission and the church in the various parts of the world. Although neat diagrams communicate clearly and graphically how many Christians there are in relation to the followers of other religions, they also oversimplify and force us to produce statistics which cannot actually be discovered. For example, we have no accurate idea of how many Christians there are in China – and this figure is large enough to influence overall figures for the world. Graphs of the growth of particular churches can misrepresent the realities of the working of God's Spirit in promoting his kingdom. While I remain grateful for the statistics, graphs and diagrams in other people's writings, the multitude of question marks I have added in the margins of such books and articles has compelled me to refuse to yield to pressures to add such aids to this book. Genuine truth must remain more important than particular styles of communication.

2

To the Jew first:
what is God doing among Jews?

Since Jesus and all the original Christians were Jews, the church is rooted in Jewish soil. With his repeated phrase 'to the Jew first' (Romans 1:16; 2:9–10), Paul, the apostle to the gentiles, underlines how vitally significant the Jews are in God's eyes. So it seems right to start our world tour with a brief chapter on what God is doing among Jews.

Behind everything that relates to Jews hangs the spectre of the Holocaust. The nightmare of the Nazi concentration camps and gas chambers haunts us. In just a few years, six million Jews, one third of the total race, died in an appalling way. Almost every European Jew today lost relatives in Hitler's genocidal horror.

Some gentile Christians ask therefore whether it can be right for them to evangelize among Jews. With the background of the Holocaust, has the church any right to preach to Jews? Christian Zionists have chosen to show friendship to the state and people of Israel, but deny the need for evangelism. They are not unique in this stance. Some other Christians note how Israel has failed to show proper justice in its dealings with the Palestinians, so they side with the Arabs against the Jews; for them Jewish evangelism is secondary to questions of political justice. Many more liberal Christians in recent years have also opposed evangelism of Jews, claiming that Jews have their own covenant and way to God. They cannot see why Jews need Jesus.

But to be faithful to their Lord, Christians must evangelize all peoples because they all, including the Jews, need the good news of Jesus, the Messiah.

Christians must evangelize

Compromise of biblical truth is never right, even if the motive is one of apparent humility and love. As Christians we need to recognize the evils which have in the past been perpetrated in the name of Christ and repent of all such anti-semitism. Nevertheless with sensitive humility we are called to share the good news which we have received and which has changed our lives. We believe that in the life, death and resurrection of Jesus Christ, God has given us not only eternal life and hope, but also a present enjoyment of his forgiving love and his life-giving Spirit. To keep such good news to ourselves and deny it to our Jewish friends would in fact be a new form of anti-semitism. As a Jewish Christian myself I felt deeply sad when a Swedish missionary to Israel attacked all evangelism among Jews and told me that I ought not to be a Christian. She believed that as

God's chosen people we Jews have no need of anything beyond the Mosaic covenant. What would Peter, Paul, James, John and other early Jewish Christians have thought if they had known that later gentile Christians would have denied them the right to have the gospel of Jesus presented to them?

Happily the God of Israel is still at work and giving both Jewish and gentile Christians a renewed vision for evangelism among Jews.

Jews need Jesus

We have already noted in the previous chapter that both Jews and gentiles are under the power of sin (Romans 3:9) and equally need the salvation which Jesus Christ has won for us in his death. Paul in Romans was assuming that Jews need the Messiah, and seeking to show that gentiles too should be evangelized. Today the boot is on the other foot. We take it for granted that the Messiah or Christ is for gentiles, but some question whether Jews should turn to him for salvation. The Bible is realistic in its assessment. Both Jews and gentiles suffer the same problem of sin. And the one God of all the world has provided in Jesus Christ the one solution to that problem.

Some Christians can be naive in their understanding of Jews. They think romantically that all Jews still follow the Old Testament faith of their fathers without any change or development. They wonder why Jews today need the atoning work of Jesus whereas Old Testament Jews could be saved without knowing who the awaited Messiah was.

Actually of course Jews today not only believe in the Hebrew Scriptures (Old Testament), but also in the whole development of rabbinic thought and particularly the Talmud. Judaism is not just the faith of the Old Testament, but has added much that is quite human. Judaism therefore fails to give us God's revealed truth in its purity and fulness. It is inadequate as a way of salvation. Jews need the Messiah both to fulfil that which is true in Judaism and to provide atonement for sin and untruth.

With the passing of time attitudes are changing. An increasing number of Jewish and gentile Christians are sharing the good news of the Messiah Jesus with Jewish neighbours and friends. It is now almost half a century since the Holocaust. Although the memory of this trauma can never be erased from Jewish minds, yet its bitterness begins to be softened as the years pass. To more and more Jews it is no longer a personal memory from their own experience. Only older people remember the nightmare. For them it is tragically hard to envisage faith in Jesus as the solution to the insecurity, bitterness and suspicion of other people which often follow the experience of persecution.

But as the Holocaust slips a little into history it has become more possible for some Orthodox Jews to face seriously the fact that Jesus is Jewish. Some searching books have been written, seeking to examine who he really was and how he fits into Jewish history. Many ordinary Jews around the world are more open today to consider the claims of Jesus if they are offered with sensitivity, loving friendship and relevance.

Who are the Jews?

The Knesset or parliament in Israel still debates the definition of a Jew. Legally, descent comes through the mother, not the father. But what rabbinic sanction must there be for a legal marriage? And can you be considered Jewish if you believe in Jesus as Messiah? Strangely no parallel question is asked of the ultra-orthodox Chassidic Jews who claim that their now dead leader, Rabbi Schnerson, is the Messiah.

It is far from easy to define who is a Jew. And it is also true that there are many different sorts of Jews. There is no such thing as a 'typical Jew'. In China there are Mandarin-speaking Chinese-looking Jews, in India and Sri Lanka there are brown-skinned Jews, the Falasha Jews from Ethiopia are black, European Jews are white. Sadly the Chinese Jewish community has almost died out and the old Indian synagogue in Cochin has great difficulty in gathering the necessary quorum for Sabbath worship. Traditionally Jews have been divided into two major groupings, Ashkenazim and Sephardim. The Ashkenazim lived in Christian lands, while the Sephardim were in Muslim and southern European countries. Their traditions and world-views differ enormously. But even within those two groupings huge differences exist. An American Jew may not see eye to eye with a French Jew, or a Yemeni with a Moroccan. What's more, Judaism consists not only of the majority Orthodox, but of various denominations. Large numbers of Jews again are not religiously practising, and some have assimilated, merging into the culture and language of the country where they live. So it is not easy in one short chapter to generalize about what God is doing among Jews. But it is encouraging to note how faith in Jesus as Messiah breaks down barriers and brings peace between Jewish Christian believers of different backgrounds – one of the marks of the kingdom of God.

Where do the eighteen million Jews live? Many assume that the majority will be in the state of Israel, but actually the four and a half million Israeli Jews are outnumbered by America's six million. Just the state of New York has some three million Jews – some have joked and called Brooklyn the new Zion. We do not know precisely how many Jews live in the former Soviet Union, but estimates climb as high as four million – just imagine the problems if they all emigrated to the state of Israel. Already there are severe housing and social problems with the many thousands who have come to Israel. Outside Israel there are three quarters of a million Jews in France, a third of a million in Britain and then there are considerable communities in South Africa, Argentina, Brazil, New Zealand and many other countries.

What about Jewish believers in Jesus?

Just ten or twenty years ago it was quite rare to meet a Jewish believer in Jesus. Today things have changed. In North America there has been a significant movement of Jews to faith in Jesus. At least fifty thousand have turned to Christ, while some put the figure considerably higher. In Israel today there are probably about five thousand members of messianic assemblies, in Britain several hundred, and there are also groups in South Africa, France and elsewhere. Some have come to faith in Jesus through the vibrant personal witness of gentile Christians, while others would never have received the gospel from a gentile and have come to the Lord through other Jewish believers. But in one way and another God is building his church among the Jewish people.

There is some controversy concerning what Jewish believers should be called. Different terms are used – Jewish Christians, messianic believers, Hebrew Christians etc. While some dislike and therefore avoid the gentile word 'Christian', the uniting central fact is that we are people who believe in Jesus as our messiah, saviour and Lord. Only secondarily do we want to emphasize that we are Jewish and of Hebrew stock.

We need therefore to distinguish carefully between religion, race and culture. Although these three factors interact and influence each other, they are different. For example, I am fully Jewish by race, Christian by faith and quite mixed in culture – culturally Jewish, but also strongly influenced by my English education and context.

Gentile churches

Scattered through gentile churches and student Christian Unions in our various countries are quite a few Jewish Christians. In some cases a whole group is clustered in the one congregation and so are able to encourage one another, but generally these Jewish believers remain alone in being both Jewish and Christian. The obvious danger is that they sink anonymously into the prevailing gentile context, thus losing their particular Jewish distinctives, their racial and cultural identity. This is sad for two reasons. First, the Jewish Christians miss out if they never manage to relate their Christian faith to their Jewish heritage. This can lead to a spiritually split personality – half Jewish and half Christian – where the two do not meet and become one. Secondly, the gentile churches miss out on all they could learn from a Jewish insight into the Scriptures and the Christian faith. By submerging their Jewishness, Jewish Christians rob the churches of much potential blessing. Happily, God is increasingly at work in this respect, for with the growing number of Jewish Christians in the churches they are beginning to stand up and be counted. But there are still many who confess that they have never told anyone in their church that they are Jews.

Messianic fellowships

Many people assume that you cannot be both a Jew and a Christian. I am often asked, 'When did you stop being a Jew?' My reply is always, 'When did you stop being English?' At other times I may be introduced as coming 'from a Jewish background', implying that as a Christian I am no longer Jewish. Thus there is an ecumenical dialogue group called the 'Council of Christians and Jews' on the assumption that the Christians will not be Jews and the Jews will not be

Christians. And indeed in their dialogue meetings it is not their custom to invite Jewish Christians to participate. They strongly oppose all evangelism among Jews, even by Jewish Christians. Sadly, George Carey, the Archbishop of Canterbury, has given strong evidence of supporting this stance.

It is a very important phenomenon in the history of evangelism among Jews that in these past few years a new movement has developed. New churches with a strong Jewish identity have sprung up not only in Israel, but also in many other countries. They are called Messianic Fellowships or Assemblies in some countries, Messianic Synagogues in America. Their existence, as strongly Jewish and yet also clearly Christian bodies, demonstrates unequivocally that it is after all possible to be both Jewish and Christian.

The Messianic Fellowships generally avoid all vocabulary which is linked in Jewish minds to a history of persecution. Thus they do not call themselves churches, but fellowships or assemblies. The name 'Christian' belonged to those who persecuted Jews and so is replaced by the term 'believer', while the concept of 'conversion', being often associated with forced conversion, is expressed in terms of 'becoming a believer'. Likewise, militaristic terminology such as 'crusades' or 'spiritual warfare', or an emphasis on power remind us of pogroms and the Holocaust. We therefore avoid them.

Jewish believers within these fellowships generally prefer to call the Lord by the Hebrew name Yeshua ha-Meshiah rather than by the gentile title Jesus Christ.

The Messianic Fellowships are struggling to find forms of worship which reflect their Jewish culture and heritage. In this there is often a blend of the vivacious and lively together with the solemn and traditional. A lively more charismatic song with Israeli dancing may yield suddenly to an old Hebrew chant. What is merely vivacious can be superficial and fail to honour the God who is inexpressibly holy and pure; what is only solemn may become boringly old-fashioned, losing sight of the incarnation of Christ which brings God close to us in an intimate personal relationship. And the joy of the Holy Spirit as a mark of God's kingdom will be clearly evident.

Inevitably there is also a tendency to see Scripture through Jewish eyes rather than by the traditional gentile approaches. Equally Christian faith is applied to the issues which lie heavily on Jewish hearts and minds. A new emphasis on Jewish approaches to the Bible and to theology is witnessed by the development of Jewish Christian theological journals like Mishkan.

In fact, through these fellowships God is renewing a form of Christianity which in many ways is more culturally akin to the church of the New Testament period. They are looking at questions which faced new Jewish believers then, particularly in their relationship to the Old Testament Law and to the increasing presence of gentiles in the church. And in these days much debate rages concerning the state of Israel in relationship to Old Testament prophecy.

As might be expected, considerable controversy exists within the Christian church concerning these fellowships. Some observe the danger that they could become exclusive and separatist. It should however be noted that at least 40 per cent of the members of the Messianic Fellowships are gentiles. Others note the possibility that they could stress their Jewishness more than their faith in Jesus as Messiah. A few feel threatened when they hear that traditional gentile interpretations of the Bible and of theology can be questioned. It is of course true that these relatively new movements may sometimes yield to such temptations, but the New Testament churches were also not without their problems. Meanwhile we cannot but rejoice at the growing stream of Jews who are becoming believers in Jesus and are beginning to relate their faith to their Jewish heritage. This makes it easier for other Jews to follow them into faith in Christ. Surely God is at work – and yet it is still only a small minority of Jews who are coming to follow the Lord.

In recent years this minority has increased considerably because of the many thousands of Jews who have left the lands of the former Soviet Union in search of greater wealth and security. This has changed the face of Jewish Christianity and of evangelism among Jews. Many of the Russian Jews have proved wide open to the gospel of Jesus Christ. As a result the Messianic Assemblies in Israel have grown in numbers and many have had to use Russian as a second language alongside Hebrew. Many Russian Jews have also set up home in other countries. Jewish evangelism in America has found a ripe harvest field among these new settlers and many have found faith in Christ. Even Germany has welcomed at least a hundred thousand Russian Jews, so Christians are having to focus attention on Berlin as a new centre for Jewish evangelism. And in the former Soviet Union itself mission work among Jews has proved abundantly fruitful.

Leading the way in Jewish evangelism is the largest Christian mission among Jews, Jews for Jesus. All its front-line workers are themselves Jews and the mission therefore exhibits a very Jewish character which causes controversy among some gentile Christians who don't like their very up-front direct methods. However, their very public evangelism and their use of large advertisements in newspapers, magazines and underground trains has put Jewish evangelism on the front burner and opened doors for other missions too in their quieter work. Happily, the different Jewish missions have worked well in fellowship and mutual cooperation together, each having their own patterns of ministry.

As Jews we rejoice in the tremendous concern that many gentile Christians have both for Israel as a land and for the Jewish people. We long that all Christians would not only show loving friendship towards Israel and Jews, but also share with us what is most precious to every Christian, namely Jesus Christ himself. Love and evangelism belong inseparably together. Love will also allow us to evangelize our own people in ways which fit us with our cultural background. And love will encourage us to develop truly Jewish patterns in the life of the church, in the understanding of the Bible and in the theological expression of our Christian faith.

3

The church's greatest challenge: what is God doing among Muslims?

We have already noted that God controls not only the lives of his church and people, but also reigns as God over all the world, holding the reins of history in his sovereign hands. Under his direction the world of Islam has changed incredibly in these past few decades. Our perception of Muslims has changed in two ways.

First, there is the significance for Muslims of the recent changes in East Europe. No longer is the West preoccupied with the communist world as its great rival. One can only ask whether the new division of power blocks will not be between Europe and America on the one side and the Muslim world on the other. Already one detects a sense of mutual fear and even hatred. To many Muslims, Americans and Europeans are a satanic foe waiting for an opportunity to destroy Islam and its followers. Equally many westerners shudder at pictures of fanatical Muslim crowds surging through city streets, and think of Muslims as militant terrorists. Racial or religious caricatures of this nature always distort truth. They also work strongly against Christian love which is a necessary prerequisite for Christian witness. How can we share the good news of grace unless we are ourselves gracious in love?

A second change in our perception is based on economics. Just 30 or 40 years ago most people had never heard of the desert oases and little fishing villages of Kuwait, Bahrain or Dubai. The Muslim world was poor and backward with little significance in the wider arenas of world economics or politics. It is hard today to believe it. Muslims are convinced that it was God who used oil to demonstrate the truth and glory of Islam. Christians too believe that the revolutionizing influence of oil was under God's sovereign control. What was his purpose? Was it to bring the two worlds of Islam and Christianity more closely together? Was it to give the church new openings for sharing the reality of God in Jesus Christ among Muslims?

Certainly it is true that the two worlds of Islam and the West have been drawn into close proximity both in western countries and in Muslim lands. Sadly they are often like oil and water – living next to each other, but without any vital relationship.

Muslims in the West frequently form little ghettos apart from their white neighbours, often disliking and disliked. The first generation can feel threatened and insecure as a minority in an alien culture. Many also struggle to learn the language. But the second generation will attend school locally and will speak the language perfectly. Some feel hemmed in and restricted by the narrow ethnic community of their parents, while others experience racial prejudice and discrimination which pushes them back into the ghetto. While the former may become more open to the Christian faith, the latter sometimes find their identity in a rather militant form of Islam.

Sadly, it remains true that in most European countries our Muslim populations find little welcome. They commonly experience racialist attitudes. This makes it harder for white Christians to share their faith meaningfully and acceptably with their Muslim neighbours. The large and dynamic black churches in our principal cities could relate more easily and thus play a significant part in the work of evangelism among Muslims.

In Muslim countries too westerners, drawn to work there by high salaries, often find that they are unable to make friendships with local people. Nevertheless the opportunity is there for Christians to observe Islam, and for Muslims to meet Christians. Because of this there is a small trickle of conversions both from Islam to Christianity and vice versa. A few years ago it was almost unthinkable that Arab Muslims in the heartlands of Islam would become Christians. But now we begin to hear of family clans turning to Jesus Christ in one or two such countries and some leading individuals too who are being converted. In western countries there is quite a flow of Muslims becoming Christians, particularly westernized second-generation young people. There is however no room for naive triumphalism in this, for it is still only a relatively very small number who are coming to faith in Christ. At the same time there is a corresponding trickle of westerners who have become disillusioned with what they have seen of Christianity and join Islam. But through the movements of history God has given Christians a new opportunity to show the beauty of God's grace in Christ to Muslims. Our lives will be seen and our words can be heard – what a challenge!

The church's response

'Please inform me of courses to help me to understand more about Islam and Christian witness among Muslims.'

'Please could you speak to our Christian Union about witness among Muslims?'

'Please could you advise me what opportunities there would be for me in mission among Muslims?'

Over these past years it has been encouraging to receive many such letters from all over the world. It seems that God has been moving by his Spirit in the church worldwide to arouse a particular concern for mission among Muslims. At the college where I teach we have had Latin American and Korean students who have been called by the Lord to work in Muslim countries. Many African students too now have a deep call to such ministry. In Africa the churches are running various courses to train their workers for witness among Muslims. This may have developed partly because in the past Muslims and Christians spread their faiths largely among the tribes which still followed their traditional tribal religions. Now this buffer between the Christian and Muslim communities has been almost entirely swallowed up by the two great world faiths. This means that Islam and Christianity confront each other directly now.

In one way or another the Holy Spirit is challenging the church to be involved in witness among Muslims. Twenty years ago the church's big missionary concern was for the communist world. Today the world of Islam has captured Christians' attention for prayer and evangelism. The current emphasis on 'unreached peoples' and the so-called '10–40 window' (areas of the world lying between 10° and 40° north of the Equator) has also concentrated missionary attention on the unevangelized Muslim world.

Witness among Muslims

In most Muslim countries it is illegal to witness to a Muslim and someone who is converted from Islam may well be killed. Freedom of religion is definitely not a Muslim concept. In such situations it is obviously singularly unwise to give any details concerning Christian mission in those lands. Unwise disclosure of information can lead to doors being closed for the gospel or to local Christians suffering severe persecution.

Muslims still shudder at the memory of the bitter Crusade wars between Christian and Muslim armies. They feel that the Christian crusading spirit was further evidenced in the long centuries of imperialism and colonialism in which Christian states dominated the world of Islam. Now in more recent

years the presence of American and European forces
in Muslim waters and even on the soil of the holy
land of Saudi Arabia seems to many Muslims like a
continuation of that history. In Muslim minds this is
also linked to American support for the state of Israel
which is anathema to Muslims. While many Christians see the hand of God at work bringing the state
of Israel to birth like a phoenix out of the ashes of the
German gas chambers, Muslims see it as a Zionist
and Christian plot against Islam.

Failing to understand Muslim sensitivities, some
Christians talk and behave unwisely. Undiscerning
support for the state of Israel without any criticism of
injustices against Palestinians does not reflect the
character of the biblical prophets who demonstrated
God's passion for holiness and justice. But it is equally
wrong to join the critics of Israel in naive support of
the Palestinians as if they were the purely innocent
sufferers. Biblically God has laid down repentance as
the precondition for the coming of his kingdom. There
will be no godly peace, righteousness and justice in
the Middle East until we see on both sides God's
miraculous gift of humble repentance.

In the very sensitive context of Islam it is vital that
Christians should be careful, humble and loving in
their witness. Insensitive or triumphalistic power-
consciousness will prove unwise and counter-
productive.

Both Jews and Muslims fear that Christian witness
is aimed at undermining their community. It is particularly important therefore that new converts
should be strongly encouraged to remain within
their family and society unless they are actually

thrown out. For this to be possible it may be necessary to develop patterns of Christian life and worship which are culturally related to a Muslim background. We are beginning to see this happen in some countries. For example, in one South Asian Muslim area several thousand Muslims have become believers in Jesus as Lord and Saviour, but have remained in their former society. Their forms of worship look outwardly quite Muslim, but they have a clear biblical and Christ-centred faith.

Such contextual approaches have raised serious questions. Could it even be right for Christians actually to call themselves 'Muslim'? The word 'Muslim' merely means someone who submits to God, so it does apply to Christians too. But good communication is not so much interested in what one says, but in what one wants people to understand. The word 'Muslim' is in practice always understood to mean someone who follows the faith of Islam. So Christians may justifiably be accused of lying if they say that they are Muslims.

But then contextual forms of Christian mission present us with other questions. How far is it right for Christians to adapt Muslim styles of prayer to our Christian faith? Might it be right for Christians from Muslim backgrounds to face the direction of Jerusalem when praying? Muslims face Mecca, Daniel faced Jerusalem. Could it be right for Christians to perform ritual washings before praying to signal our need to come with clean hands into God's holy presence? In Christian worship should we prostrate ourselves and follow the Muslim ritual movements in prayer, but with a Christ-centred content?

We believe that God not only took on human form in the incarnation of Jesus Christ, but he also entered a very specific culture and background as a Jew of the first century. Jesus Christ therefore gives us a model of cultural identification and adaptation – and yet without sin. We too therefore want to adapt fully to the Muslim contexts into which we come, but we long also to maintain an uncompromised witness of holiness and truth. This balance is not an easy one.

Christian witness among Muslims faces very particular hurdles. Muslims are confident that their faith is God's ultimate revelation of truth, utterly superior to everything else. With the further confidence that they are following God's way and that he will reward them for their obedience to his will, it is easy for pride to enter in. Such pride is often linked to a militancy and rigid legalism which allows only limited freedom to non-Muslims and encourages violence towards Muslims who convert to Christianity. In such circumstances a church – planting ministry becomes discouragingly difficult. Christian workers among Muslims need persevering faith which goes on trusting God despite many discouragements.

Enormous challenges

1. North Africa

My wife and I were thrilled to visit the impressive ruins of many old churches in Tunisia. We saw where Augustine had preached in the fourth century, but some of the ruins were much earlier than that. The remains of many huge churches witnessed to the great size of the Christian church in North Africa during those early centuries. But we sensed too the bitterness of the Christian church's defeat at the hands of the Muslim armies. Even the church buildings had been dismantled to provide building materials for new mosques. Today there are perhaps only about a hundred indigenous Christians, not counting the few hundred foreign Protestant Christians and about fifteen to twenty thousand Roman Catholics living in Tunisia.

Under the onslaughts of the Muslim armies and mass emigration, conversions to Islam and finally a terrible plague, the church gradually declined and died in North Africa west of Egypt. Islam stands triumphant and Christian witness is tough. The few Christian converts face tremendous pressure from their families, at work and in society. They are often imprisoned or harassed by the police. Over the years some have been poisoned or otherwise martyred for their faith. And yet today these little fellowships of local Christians are gradually growing – God is at work, although it is hardly revival.

One area of considerable growth for the Christian faith has been among the Kabyle people in Algeria. The Kabyle are the original inhabitants of the land before the Arabs conquered and settled. Several thousand have turned to the Lord and living churches have been formed. The Kabyle are closely related to the Berbers across the border in Morocco. The Moroccan Berbers have often shown their longing for genuine identity by starting new movements of popular mystical Islam. How wonderful it would be to see the gospel spread through the Kabyle to the Berbers! In Jesus Christ they could indeed find a new sense of worth and ethnic identity.

When my wife and I were visiting in south Egypt we observed the same search for identity among the Nubians. The Nubians had a strong Christian civilization for many centuries and it is only a few hundred years ago that they finally succumbed to Islam. But in Egypt they are looked down on as second-class citizens because of the dark colour of their skin. The gospel of Jesus Christ can give us all a new understanding of our dignity and value in the sight of God.

While Saudi Arabia is the religious heart of Islam, Egypt has always been the intellectual and theological centre. The Muslim Brotherhood, the foundation of the Islamist/fundamentalist movement in modern Islam, began in Egypt and still has its base there. Thousands of Muslim missionaries gain their training in Cairo before fanning out all over the world to spread the message of Islam. What happens in Egypt has strategic importance therefore for the whole development of the Muslim world.

Unlike the North African countries to the west of Egypt, in Egypt itself the Christian church has withstood the long centuries of Muslim pressure and discrimination. The original Coptic Orthodox Church claims about ten per cent of the population as its members, but many estimate that as many as 17 per cent may actually be Christians. The church has survived partly by keeping a low profile without aggravating the Muslim authorities by witnessing to their Muslim neighbours. But today there are some

Coptic Orthodox Christians who are gaining a vision of discreet but active witness among Muslims – and some are being converted as a result.

Out of the Orthodox church various Protestant churches have come into being, particularly the Presbyterian Synod of the Nile. They also share the task of bringing the gospel to the majority Muslim population. In this delicate task it is vital to combine wisdom with boldness, boldness with wisdom.

2. *Turkey and Turkic peoples*

Straddling the two continents of Europe and Asia stands the huge country of Turkey. Through the influence of Ataturk it became a secular state despite the fact that its population of over sixty million people is almost entirely Muslim. But in more recent years strongly traditional Islam has been gaining ground and has entered the highest level of government. But at the same time Turkey's desire to be an integral part of the European Union requires it to maintain democracy with considerable political freedoms.

In the past there were large minority Christian churches among the Assyrians, Greeks and Armenians. Sadly however, vicious persecution has led not only to the slaughter of many of these Christians, but also now to a mass emigration to America and other countries. But some remain and we are encouraged to observe a renewal of spiritual life particularly in the Armenian Orthodox Church.

Over the past couple of decades a growing number of expatriate Christian workers have witnessed effectively among the Turks themselves. As a result various indigenous fellowships have come to life and today there are several hundred Turkish Christians. And this number is growing steadily. In the past Turkish believers were severely harassed and even persecuted, but today it has become a little easier generally.

All across the former Soviet Central Asia right into northern China live various peoples who are closely related to the Turkish people and speak similar languages. In this area Islam claims some sixty million followers.

Until relatively recently under the Communist power of the Soviet Union, very little could be done by western Christians to bring the gospel of Jesus Christ to them. But now the more open political situation has opened a door for more Christians from other countries to take professional jobs in those areas and quietly share the gospel. Local Russian Christians too continue to be engaged in bold witness among their Muslim neighbours. Bible translation and the production of Christian literature in local languages has begun. Many are coming to faith in Jesus Christ and new Christian fellowships are springing up. This is particularly true in Kazakhstan, but to a lesser degree also in Uzbekistan and the other Central Asian republics.

Under Stalin, many German communities from the Ukraine were forcibly moved into the remote and inhospitable areas where these Muslim peoples live. Many of the Germans were Christian and they formed their own churches. Sadly most of them were content merely to survive as Christians and had little

vision for the evangelization of their Muslim neighbours – and in the fearfully dark days of Stalinist
oppression none of us can criticize them for this. Since
Gorbachev, greater freedom has reigned, and it has
been easier for them to share their faith openly. But
this same freedom also allows the Christians to move,
and about a hundred thousand have left the area,
emigrating to America, Israel or Germany. Since the
German emigration also included many Jews, this has
given new growth and impetus to the messianic fellowships of Israel and America, but it has seriously
weakened the witness of the gospel in Central Asia.

Today the countries of Central Asia find themselves the object of very considerable Islamic pressure
from Saudi Arabia, Pakistan and Turkey. Foreign
money flows in for the building of beautiful new
mosques and the import of large quantities of
Qur'ans. In the past before the coming of Communism these peoples were solidly Muslim, so a search
for their true roots and for national identity goes hand
in hand with a resurgence of Islam. On the other hand
the Central Asian governments and leaders seem well
aware of the dangers of Islamic fundamentalism and
therefore resist any extremes. But the growth of Islam
is beginning to make it harder for Christian workers
to have an open witness in some of these countries.

Under Communism the Christian church suffered
fierce persecution, but still persisted in its witness.
Thus one old grandmother told me how she would
ride all day on a crowded bus and preach to those
standing around her. When I asked her what reac-
tions she got, she was surprised that I should ask such
a stupid question.

'Just like in the New Testament, of course', she replied. 'Some believed and some rejected the gospel.'

She told me how some people spat in her face, others elbowed her or hit her – but others came to saving faith in Jesus Christ.

So the Baptist and Pentecostal churches held on through those days of suffering, but they became increasingly legalistic and rigid. It has not been easy for them to relate to the more open society in which they now bear their witness. But still they have grown markedly and have also planted new congregations in the main cities.

Meanwhile a multitude of foreign workers have flooded into Central Asia, each planting churches of their own type. Extreme charismatic churches with prosperity theology have multiplied. Then other charismatic churches have been planted – and non-charismatic churches, anti-charismatic churches, 'evangelical' churches, churches with particular views on legalism, various Korean denominations ... churches of every sort have sprung up among the Russians and most have flourished.

Among the Muslim indigenous populations too a whole variety of fellowships have come into being. Thus in Almaty, the capital of Kazakhstan, there are at least thirty Christian fellowships among the Kazakh people. These are generally to some extent contextualized to the local Muslim background.

While one rejoices to see so many people coming to faith in Jesus Christ and beginning to enjoy the riches of eternal life in him, it is also sad to observe the grave disunity and empire-building pride exhibited by the host of Christian workers from overseas.

3. The Middle East

Because the prophet Mohammed was an Arab and the Qur'an was written in Arabic, the Arabs will always remain the key to the world of Islam. While Indonesia is the country with the largest number of Muslims and there are more Muslims in India, Pakistan or Bangladesh than in any Middle East country, nevertheless the bloodstream of Islam flows out from Saudi Arabia, Egypt and the Middle East.

It would be an unwise prophet who sought to foretell the future of this turbulent area. It was early in 1990, just before Iraq's invasion of Kuwait, that the Pentagon stated that the Middle East was no longer in the centre of world attention.

They said that Eastern Europe was now centre stage in the political and economic world, whereas the Middle East had lost significance! Just as the politics of the region bubble constantly in a turmoil of uncertainty, so also it is hard to predict the future developments of Islam. Will fundamentalism win the day and bring in the fullness of Islamic law? Or will the divisions in the world of Islam cause some disillusionment? Might it be that somehow the rock-like fortress of Islam will begin to crack and yield converts in large numbers to Christian witness? There are at least some signs of a growing openness among some to read the Bible and in many countries a few people are finding their painful way to faith in Jesus Christ. But the fortress remains impressively strong.

In these days of easy travel and the growth of information technology, Muslim leaders in the Middle East find it increasingly difficult to shield their people from the Bible and Christian witness. As was the case in Communist countries in former years, so now in the Middle East the rigorous examinations of customs officials still fail to prevent Bibles being brought into these countries. Personal computers multiply portions of the Bible, cassettes are reproduced and God's word spreads. When Arabs travel to visit other countries where freedom of religion is greater, they often return with the goods they cannot obtain at home – whisky, pornography and the Bible. Christians pray that the right spirit will prevail! May God's word come with fresh and vital power by the Holy Spirit!

Thanks to oil money enormous development has come to the various states in the Middle East. This has necessitated a huge influx of foreign workers – experts from America and Europe, blue-collar workers from Egypt and Asia, maids from the Philippines to serve in the homes of the wealthy. In some of the Gulf States the majority of the population are overseas workers. Inevitably a proportion will be Christians and some of them will have come in order to share their faith locally. Most of the Philippino maids come from a very traditional background of corrupted Roman Catholicism, but they believe in a God who heals miraculously. Living right in the homes of the top people they are subject to terrible abuse, but they also have the opportunity to demonstrate the reality of a God who answers prayer for healing.

While in the Arabian peninsula Christian witness is dependent on foreign workers, in Jordan, Iraq, Iran and Syria we also have the ancient Orthodox churches plus a few Protestants who have largely come out from the Orthodox churches. We need to pray and work for these ancient churches that their witness may be effective and fruitful.

4. *The Indian sub-continent*

India – 110 million Muslims; Pakistan – 130 million Muslims; Bangladesh – 115 million Muslims; Afghanistan – 17 million Muslims. In our concern for witness among Muslims we dare not overlook these huge populations. Pakistan and Bangladesh are moving steadily towards a fuller implementation of Islamic law. As the Taliban fundamentalists gain control of most of Afghanistan, they too implement a rigid application of Islamic law to every area of life. People are being strung up on lamp-posts and executed just for possessing a Bible. Only Hindu India is free from these pressures, although here too the Muslim population would like to have Muslim law for their own community and thus form almost a state within a state. Wherever Islamic law has power, it is particularly hard to communicate the Christian gospel. Witness to Muslims becomes strictly illegal and conversion from Islam to another religion can be punishable by death. The church will be marginalized and deprived of many of its rights. For example, it becomes almost impossible to obtain permission to build new churches or to have any open witness.

But in each of these countries there is a growing interest among some Christians in sharing the gospel with their Muslim compatriots. Much new thinking is being done on how to witness among Muslims and what should be the forms of worship and church life among new converts. The result has been that some Muslims have begun to understand the gospel more clearly and hearing has led to faith.

Particularly in Bangladesh and India we have seen a growth of new contextualized churches which relate closely to the cultural background of the Muslim society. Inevitably this raises difficult questions as to how much of the Muslim background can be carried over into the Christian church. For example, should men and women worship together? And what is the role of women in the Christian church and society?

While Bangladesh is in many ways more easygoing than Pakistan and therefore more tolerant of Christian witness, it has its own problems. Owing to the horrendous floods and natural disasters which have struck Bangladesh, many relief workers have poured in to bring aid to the needy. As is often the case, Christians have been in the forefront. As a result Bangladeshi Christians have sometimes been tempted to become passive recipients of help from outside, viewing mission workers as God's channels of money and material goods. A beggar mentality will never lead to strong Christian churches. The theories about supplying aid and relief do not always prove so simple in practice, but it is important to develop ways of giving our expertise and assistance without superiority. In spite of such problems we are seeing Muslims becoming believers in Christ in Bangladesh. Just recently on a visit to Dacca, I rejoiced when someone told me that two leading Muslims had come to faith in Christ that day.

But what about Christian witness in the horrors of war-torn Afghanistan? The capital city of Kabul is a fearful sight with large areas totally flattened and every building throughout the city in some way damaged. The civil war between rival Muslim factions has left almost two million dead and up to four and a half million refugees. All journalists, radio and television personnel left Afghanistan during the worst of the fighting, so it remained almost unreported in western media. But Christian workers stayed throughout the troubles to help in the fearful suffering of the people there. As a result, Christians have gained a high reputation. But Islam is deeply entrenched in Afghan life and thought. It is not at all easy for people to leave Islam and become Christians, although many are disillusioned with Islam. And the excesses of the fundamentalist Taliban will surely increase their sense that Islam cannot bring the love and peace which are so desperately needed.

5. East and South-east Asia

Islam penetrated the lands of East Asia as long ago as the twelfth century and gradually spread through Indonesia, Malaysia and into the Philippines. For a while it looked as if Islam might become the predominant religion of that part of the world. But the military might and trading skills of the European powers stemmed the advance of Islam. As a result the Philippines became a largely Roman Catholic country, although the southern island of Mindanao is predominantly Muslim. The peoples of Mindanao still feel that Islam should have been the ruling religion of the whole country and bitter fighting has continued for some years there. They would really like to gain their independence or at least autonomous self-rule. But today the island of Mindanao not only houses these Muslim peoples, but also a large population of other racial groups who are not Muslims. It would therefore not be easy to impose Muslim law.

Among the indigenous churches as well as among various foreign workers God has given a deep desire to share the good news of Jesus Christ with Muslims. It is challenging to see how some local believers knowingly risk martyrdom in order to bring the gospel to Muslim communities. Some have dared to live right in Muslim villages, constantly facing the danger of murder. But in this way Muslims can see the reality of the Christian faith and the beauty of the Christian life.

The population of Malaysia is divided between Malay Muslims, Indians and Chinese. There are dynamic growing churches among the Indians and Chinese with strong well-trained Christian leaders. But the government is in the hands of Malays and considerable privileges are granted to Malays. All evangelism among Muslims is illegal and converts to Christianity face very considerable problems and persecution. If the government becomes aware that a Christian is witnessing to Malays, prison and even torture can result.

Nevertheless, we hear of a steady trickle of Malays coming to faith in Jesus Christ and a growing number of Malaysian Christians daring quietly to share their faith with Muslim friends.

In Indonesia the facts concerning the conversion of Muslims are carefully concealed lest we provoke even greater reaction against the church from conservative Muslims. But over the years the churches have grown rapidly. In former times large numbers of Christians were to be found in all the white-collar professions and even in government. Today they have been pushed to one side by Muslims and Islam has become strongly dominant. There have also been outbreaks of violence with Muslims burning churches and manses. The police seem to do nothing to protect the Christians.

The Christian church is however so large and strong that the message of the gospel is widely disseminated throughout the population. Unlike most Muslim countries, in Indonesia the basic facts of the gospel are known to many. Bibles and Christian literature in Indonesian are easily available. In most parts of Indonesia there are Christian churches, so people can observe Christians in their daily lives. Possibilities for wise witness therefore abound.

6. *Europe and North America*

Multitudes of Muslims have come to live in North America and western Europe. This has caught the church by surprise and still today few church leaders have much idea how to help their members to relate to Muslim neighbours or witness to their faith. But over these past few years many helpful books have been written on this subject and a variety of courses and seminars have taken place to teach ordinary Christians at least the basics. Former missionaries overseas have returned to their home countries and become involved in witness here. And a growing number of missionaries from Korea, Finland and other countries are coming to help us. Increasingly, Christians are responding to the call of the Lord to dedicate their lives to mission among Muslims.

Sadly, racialism and cultural insensitivity have deepened the chasm between the Muslim communities and their white neighbours. Despite the multitude of black churches and other ethnic Christian groups, the Christian faith is largely linked in Muslim minds to the white community, so religion becomes a racial affair. This adds an unfortunate feeling of bitterness. But still some younger Muslims want to relate easily with the host culture. They make friends among local people, feel attracted to European ways and some become Christians.

Muslim societies in each of these different parts of the world present a huge and formidable barrier to the spread of the gospel. But God is quietly drawing a few to faith in Jesus Christ.

As Muslims in the West get converted and become mature as Christians, they will share their faith with their families back in their home countries. And some will return to Muslim countries to bring the gospel to their own people.

What means does God use to bring Muslims to salvation in Jesus Christ? As I have elaborated in *Islam and Christian Witness*, genuine loving friendship is of primary importance. Personal relationships are of supreme significance in Muslim cultures, so it is vital that we develop long-term friendships. Then many Muslim converts have been moved by the reading of the Bible. Scripture distribution can play a vital role in witness among Muslims. Christians need to look for opportunities to lend or give the Bible or New Testament to Muslim friends. Muslims often believe strongly in dreams and visions. In his grace God meets us all in ways which fit our expectations and it is quite common to hear former Muslims testify of their conversion through a dream or vision. And then quite a few Muslims have found eternal life after experiencing a miraculous healing in the name of Jesus Christ.

The church – God's chosen instrument

In many Muslim lands Christian churches have survived long centuries of discrimination. Thus around ten per cent of the population of Egypt is Christian, largely belonging to the ancient Coptic Orthodox Church which looks back to the apostle Mark as its founder. Five per cent of Jordan, eight per cent of Syria and three or four per cent of Iraq stand out as Christians in the midst of Muslim populations. Large numbers of Arabs and Palestinians in Israel and Lebanon are also Christians. So too in Asia, Christian churches live on as witnesses to Jesus Christ – many millions of Indonesians, seven or eight per cent of Malaysia, two per cent of Pakistan, a tiny half per cent in Bangladesh and a mere handful in Afghanistan. In Muslim Africa too Christian churches exist as potential beacons of light for their Muslim neighbours. We need to pray for our sisters and brothers in lands like Gambia, Senegal, Mali and Somalia.

In such Muslim situations it is easy for Christians to develop a sense of inferiority, aiming to survive rather than to witness and grow. Fear often replaces

the joyful but humble boldness which should characterize Christians.

In country after country, signs are emerging of a
new life and vision among the ancient churches.
Although mission from outside plays a vital role in
witness, the key to evangelism must always be the
national church. It is good to see growing numbers
of foreign Christians taking jobs in Muslim countries
with the specific aim of evangelism and of forming
new Christian fellowships. More and more of these
workers have been in their adopted lands long
enough to have learned the language and culture
reasonably well. They have also formed long-term
friendships which allow a deeper and more personal
sharing of the faith.

There is however a danger that these foreign
Christian workers can bypass the national churches
in their fervent desire to evangelize and plant new
fellowships. Some are tempted to despise local Christians because they do not yet have the same passion
for Muslim evangelism or because their forms of life
and worship are so different. Christian workers need
patiently to win the respect of local churches and so
gain the right to share their vision with them. It is
arrogant to think that we alone are God's chosen
instruments to bring the gospel to Muslims in other
peoples' countries.

While we encourage and pray for foreign 'tent-
makers', let us not forget the national churches. May
God also raise up Christian workers to go to Muslim
countries with the specific aim of teaching and training within these national churches. God can use expatriate Christians to bring new life and vision.

4

A new heart for the Christian church: what is God doing in Africa?

While the Christian church has declined in Europe until it represents a minority of the overall population, in black Africa the Christian faith has captured the multitudes. The graph of church growth in tropical Africa would seem to indicate that these countries could become Christian nations in the near future; but such prognoses may actually be over-optimistic, for there is a hard core of unresponsive people, particularly Muslim minorities, in each nation. But the fact remains that the heartlands of Christianity are no longer to be found in Europe, but rather in the southern hemisphere and particularly in Africa.

In terms of world faiths, the continent of Africa divides into different regions. North of the Sahara lie the strongly Muslim Arab countries which we have already briefly looked at in the previous chapter. South of the Sahara and halfway down Sudan the population moves from being Arabs to black

Africans; and Islam begins to yield to Christianity as the predominant religion. At first there is a mixture of faiths – part of the population being Christian and part Muslim. But as we progress further south the different countries become increasingly Christian. Finally, in southern Africa, we find a belt of largely Christian nations. This includes the troubled but richly endowed land of South Africa with its background of racial tension and violence.

Maurice Sinclair in his book *Ripening Harvest, Gathering Storm* (1988)[1], as also many more recent books, shows the burgeoning growth of the Christian churches in the continent of Africa. He says that 44 per cent of all Africans profess to be Christians, even if you include the strongly Muslim north – and that figure has grown in the intervening years. It used to be said that Christianity was so tied to imperialism and colonialism that with national independence the church would wither and die. The reverse has happened, for actually the heart of the church was firmly rooted in Africa and the spread of the gospel through the continent came largely through the vital witness of ordinary African Christians and native evangelists. Since the collapse of colonialism in the 1960s the church has mushroomed in sub-Saharan Africa. Strong and gifted church leaders have developed, evangelism and mission have flourished.

The growth of the churches has however not been matched by a corresponding social and economic development. In various countries, drought has reduced the land to desert conditions, so that the Sahara has crept inexorably southwards. With the drought has come fearful famine, pictures of which have stirred the hearts and generosity of many of us as we have watched television. The ghastly tragedy of mass starvation is a deeply disturbing reality which makes the weight-conscious western societies appear a sick mockery. In these next years the West must find a way to share its food mountains with the starving.

Massive urbanization plus the grave decline of African economies is causing degrading poverty. And international capital has lost patience with much of black Africa and is therefore very hesitant to invest. Slums with minimum or no sanitation sprawl around the edges of Africa's fast-growing cities and towns. Men have often gone to the cities in search of work and money, leaving their wives and children to tend the fields at home. This leads not only to the breakdown of family life with consequent moral problems, but also to a sense of hopelessness, underdevelopment and poverty in country areas too.

In the light of such immense economic needs, it is a double tragedy to see the continent torn by strife and war. Hard-earned and desperately needed national resources are squandered to buy arms. Country after country has been devastated by civil war. The formerly prosperous and educated Uganda was ruined in the struggles connected with Idi Amin. Many of the educated and professional classes were eliminated and now the nation faces an uphill battle. Drought-ridden Ethiopia and Sudan have suffered long years of bitter warfare. The horrendous bloodshed of civil war in Liberia and Sierra Leone defies description. The former Portuguese colonies, Angola and Mozambique, have been torn apart by savage fighting. Inter-tribal slaughter has devastated Rwanda and Burundi, while the Republic of Congo (Zaire) is likewise in danger of falling apart.

Now in more recent years a new scourge threatens to overwhelm black Africa – AIDS. In such countries as Zambia, Uganda, Rwanda and Congo this has reached epidemic proportions, threatening to wipe out whole sections of the population. In recent satellite pictures of some parts of those areas the whole colouring has changed, for the forest has taken over where AIDS has depopulated whole villages. No longer is AIDS just the result of sexual promiscuity, for now it is so widespread that many children are born with the disease. Missionaries and the national churches are in the forefront of this desperate battle. So far it has to be said that their teaching on sexual morality has borne only limited fruit, but ultimately this is the only way to check the wide spread of AIDS. Christians also lead the field in Africa in providing loving care for those who are slowly dying because of AIDS. In their fear and dire need many people are finding solace and new life in Christ and in fellowship within his church, but as Christians this does not soften the heartache as we 'weep with those who weep' (Rom. 12:15) because of AIDS.

Optimism

Anyone who has spent time in black Africa will have sensed the amazing cheerful optimism and warm humour which generally characterize African cultures. The emotionally reserved and often negatively pessimistic European may view this positive and open-hearted approach as somewhat naive, but it contains a genuineness which shames the sophisticated facades of the West. We cannot but admire such optimism which persists despite the droughts, famines, poverty, injustice, wars and AIDS which we have just described.

This optimism is closely linked to an innate spirituality which underlies the whole worldview. Even outwardly Marxist Africans in Angola or other countries generally retain a basic awareness of spiritual realities. While almost every African people has a traditional belief in a High God who is also creator of the world, in practice a whole host of lesser spirits has been added to supplement the often rather remote High God. Mother Earth, nature and ancestral spirits abound in the African pantheon. In everyday life it is these spirits which can heal sickness, protect from curses and harm, help with the crops or enable a woman to have a baby. Even when people become Christians or Muslims they frequently revert to their traditional spirit practices when faced with sickness, death or other tragedies. A veneer of Islam or Christianity may sometimes cover a heart which remains rooted in African traditional religion.

But it is also this fundamental spirituality which makes so many Africans so receptive to the message of Jesus Christ.

African spirituality is usually expressed through dynamic music and dance. When visiting Africa I am always struck by the way even very young children seem naturally and spontaneously to dance to the music and clap in time with the syncopated beat. It is therefore interesting to note how many African churches have adapted quite traditional western hymns and given them a more African rhythm. Staid and unemotional worship hardly fits an African context, although traditional forms mean much to both Muslims and Christians.

African spiritual awareness is also often expressed by a clear and open relationship with God personally which leads to considerable prayerfulness. In the college where I teach we are often put to shame by our African students who may spend long hours in prayer each day while as Europeans we may struggle to have a regular half-hour devotional time. When one is in Africa, relationship with God seems much less complicated and more natural. People also talk very freely and without embarrassment about God and about spiritual realities. God is so much part of everything in daily life that it would be strange not to talk about him in normal conversation.

The church

It is always unwise to generalize about a whole continent as if there were no difference between the various countries. Actually of course each nation and people is distinct. And there are enormous differences between West Africa and East Africa. History too has left an indelible mark. French, Portuguese, British, German, Belgian and Spanish colonialism each introduced different forms of education, politics and culture which endure even while reaction against colonialism burns strongly.

This is also true of the church. In French-speaking Africa, the Roman Catholic church is often relatively strong while Protestantism may be very weak. But this is not always the case, for the Republic of Congo (Zaire), Rwanda and Burundi abound with a multitude of Protestant churches of various types. In English-speaking countries Protestant churches are often very strong indeed. These will include the traditional denominations, but others may also have taken deep root. Thus the inter denominational missions in many countries have formed strong churches which are now major denominations. In East Africa the non-denominational Africa Inland Mission has brought to birth the Africa Inland Church, which in Kenya is as large as the Anglican church. In Ethiopia the Sudan Interior Mission has left behind a dynamic church which is the largest Protestant denomination in the country and has had a vital witness in spite of fierce government persecution. In West Africa the Sudan Interior Mission and the former Sudan United Mission can praise God for the large and dynamic churches they have brought into existence. Other missions too have played their part in God's missionary task of forming independent national churches which are strong in faith and witness.

But there is a danger. In spite of the fact that in theory the various African churches are now indigenous and independent of foreign domination, in practice this is not always the case. The poverty of many African churches makes it easy for rich western churches to gain undue power through financial assistance. Money can easily have strings attached. The principal of one African theological college told me that he did not agree with the official teaching of his college on the second coming of Christ and on polygamy. When I remonstrated that he was the head of the whole college and presumably therefore had some say in these matters, he disagreed. If the college's sponsors in America discovered that the principal gave teaching which they did not approve of, they would withdraw support and the college would be bankrupt. Because of the dangers of such economic imperialism, one African bishop said to me that western churches need to give much more sacrificially in order to receive the Lord's blessing, but for the sake of the African churches it would be better if their money got lost in the ocean before it arrived in Africa! True – and yet untrue! For the churches need help both in finance and in professional skills – in medicine, agriculture, education, Bible teaching and leadership training. The vital question is how western experts can assist the national churches, and how financial aid can be given without paternalism and without gaining control or undue influence over the development of the churches.

In more recent years we see some Asian missionaries, Chinese and Korean, struggling with these same issues. They also come to Africa with much financial wealth, high levels of education and top professional skills. But sometimes they are not aware of the dangers of a new form of imperialism.

Revival

'Hello! I'm so happy to meet you. My name is Joseph and I was a fearful sinner and lost in my rebellion against the Lord. And then on 3 June 1983 I met Jesus Christ and God saved me. Praise the Lord!'

I met Joseph when going for a walk one day and it was just a brief, casual encounter. The East African revival has influenced even everyday greetings and I had to learn to share a short testimony of that sort both before speaking or preaching and also when meeting people. This revival movement has been burning now for over sixty years and has deeply influenced the whole life of the churches in East Africa. It started and is still centred in the Anglican churches, but its vitality has spread more widely now. While at first it was not in any way related to the more recent charismatic movement, now it contains within itself both charismatic and non-charismatic tendencies. The chief characteristic of this burning movement of God's Spirit has been a deep and open repentance. National Christians and missionaries alike have been moved to open confession of sin which has led to true reconciliation and often to humble, loving relationships.

As always with the work of the Holy Spirit weaknesses can easily undermine the beauties of God's working. Confession of sin can become just another traditional form. Christians can become proud of their confession and repentance. Renewed Christians can feel superior to other believers and disunity between charismatic and non-charismatic threatens the life of the whole renewal movement. And yet in his grace the Lord continues to overrule human sin and pride. The work of the life-giving Holy Spirit burns on.

In West Africa in more recent years a new evangelistic and missionary vision has broken into the churches. Already thirty years ago, some churches joined together to initiate united evangelistic outreach not only to the followers of tribal religion, but also to their Muslim neighbours. This led to some churches growing significantly and a new enthusiasm capturing the hearts of many Christians. Some years ago a former student of the college where I teach formed a missionary society in the Nigerian churches to which he belonged. He has the vision of bringing the good news of Jesus Christ to those racial groups which previously had no Christian witness. His missionary society now has over seven hundred active members, most of whom are witnessing in tribes in Nigeria itself, but a few also work across the borders in other countries.

As we have already noted, Muslims and Christians are increasingly having to relate to each other. This has proved particularly tense in northern Nigeria where violence has led to the murder of many Christians and the burning down of various church buildings. Muslims have wanted to turn Nigeria officially into a Muslim nation, but this has been rightly resisted by the large Christian population. While the north of Nigeria is predominantly Muslim, the south is largely Christian. Christians therefore form about 50 per cent of the population. But the large churches formed through the interdenominational missions are particularly active in the centre and north of the country, while the old traditional denominations have their centres in the south.

While in Nigeria the interaction of Muslims and Christians has led to such fearful violence, in many other countries this has not been the case. Thus in countries like Gambia, Senegal or Mali, fundamentalist forms of Islam have not been well received by the local population. There the Muslims can seem more African than Muslim. For example, the womens' dress styles reveal a bare shoulder and so hardly conform to Islamic law! And women may be seen washing topless in the river with men walking nonchantly past – Saudi Arabians would find this hard to believe!

The development of the church in Mali could prove strategic both for wider witness among black Africans and also to reach north across their borders into Algeria and Mauritania. Although the church numbers less than a hundred thousand members, it is well established with good leadership. And many Muslims in Mali are more open than their co-religionists in other Muslim areas. This may be because large sections of the population are still relatively new Muslims, only recently converted to Islam from their traditional tribal faiths.

In the west of Mali there are many Mauritanians who live and work on the Mali side of the border. Some of these are still slaves, for Mauritanian Islam still practises slavery and there were slave markets even as late as 1979. There are almost no Christians in Mauritania and it is only very recently that a few expatriate Christian workers have begun to gain a foothold in that country. So it may be that through witness in Mali the gospel could reach across the border into the almost closed land of Mauritania.

Across the border in Senegal we again find that many Muslims are relatively open to the gospel of Christ. In a total population of about nine million some six per cent are Christian. Through the translation work of the Wycliffe Bible Translators the Christian faith is seen to relate to the various tribes, whereas Islam communicates only in the main Wolof language or in Arabic. While WBT relates closely to other missions which can do the work of evangelism and church planting, it is important too that the WBT teams should also be active in evangelism.

Throughout black Africa a multitude of new movements has mushroomed into existence. Generally these have been called 'Independency Churches'. Some of them resemble more traditional Protestant or Catholic churches with beliefs which are largely in line with accepted Christian faith. Others are so closely akin to animistic tribal religion that other Christians cannot accept them as true churches. Most of them fall somewhere between these two ends of the spectrum. All of them are very African culturally. The majority have developed as splits from traditional Protestant churches, although a few have come out from the Roman Catholic church.

They vary in size from the enormous Church of Simon Kimbangu which has its centre in the Republic of Congo and claims at least five million members down to a wide variety of tiny little groups all over black Africa.

What has led to this multiplication of Independency churches? Often they were started by a dynamic leader who had a life-changing spiritual experience, but found his or her charisma and leadership gifts were not given adequate scope to be used in the traditional churches. He/she would perhaps notice that some aspect of teaching in the Bible was omitted or underplayed in that church. For example, I remember visiting an Independency church in Kenya where the leader felt the traditional churches failed to praise the Lord 'with loud clashing cymbals' (Ps. 150:5) and so reacted against the whole western-ized worship patterns of the church. Their worship was accompanied by metal rods beating loudly on metal brake drums from old lorries – and it certainly was loud! And it was 'clashing'!

The Independency churches tend to foster a strong sense of belonging. Like the vibrant music and the dynamic leadership model this also fits the African context. As Kenneth Kaunda of Zambia has ob-served, 'Africa's gift to human culture must be in the sphere of human relationships'. The theologian John Mbiti has noted the increasing breakdown of tribal communities and therefore has urged the church to become 'the new tribe'.

The Independency churches often practise mi-raculous healing, spiritual gifts like tongues and ex-orcism of evil spirits. In this way they touch the deeper recesses of the African soul which are some-times ignored by traditional churches which can be too western in character. Unfortunately the fearful lack of adequate Bible teaching often allows unChris-tian excesses and almost animistic practices.

In more recent years, a new movement has fol-lowed in the footsteps of the Independency churches. A wide variety of independent charismatic churches have sprung up, particularly among the middle classes in the cities.

Just as the Independency church movement had its origins in South Africa, so also the development of independent charismatic churches, has had a major impact on the Christian church in South Africa. Large churches with prosperity theology have come into being in several of the main cities. Vineyard churches have drawn large numbers to their congregations too. These churches have mainly attracted middle class whites, but good numbers of so-called coloured people (those of mixed race) have also joined them.

Each racial group in South Africa has had its own particular forms of church life. The Dutch-background Afrikaaners have inevitably developed the Reformed denominations which were common in Holland, while the English-background whites have imported the various churches known in England. Black Africans have not only split into a multitude of Independency churches, but have also inherited all the denominations introduced by the white population. Like the black Africans, the Indians too have taken over the church groupings of their white neighbours.

In the days of apartheid the Dutch Reformed church was a strong bastion in support of racial segregation. But in the latter years of apartheid the church stood out in opposition and actually declared racial separation a sin and a heresy. The Anglican church also took a firm stand against all racial discrimination and Archbishop Desmond Tutu became an internationally-known figure.

The land of South Africa abounds in natural wealth with great mineral riches as well as abundant agriculture. The immense beauty of the country has the potential to attract large numbers of tourists. South Africa should be the economic hub for the development of the whole continent, but unfortunately this is not yet the case.

The days of racial segregation have left a legacy of grave social divisions, poverty-stricken black townships and inadequate economic structures. When apartheid ended and miraculously the country moved peacefully into a new multiracial society, everyone hoped that the whole country would move forward into greater prosperity, better housing for the black population and good education for all. It has not been easy to fulfil that dream. The rand has fallen dramatically against other currencies, the economy has faltered, violence has spiralled and many blacks feel impatient at the slow progress towards decent living conditions.

But the churches continue to flourish, particularly among the blacks. There is a rich variety of Bible schools and theological faculties for the training of Christian leaders. And indeed the South African churches have produced quality Christian leaders.

If South Africa could influence into the continent from the south, the large and dynamic churches of Kenya, Uganda and Tanzania in the east, and Nigeria and Ghana in the west could also play vital roles in mission throughout the continent. And in the north, Africa has the great churches of Ethiopia and Sudan.

While Ethiopia is racially different from other African peoples and stands somewhat uncomfortably between the Arabs to the north and the black Africans to the south, many throughout the continent look up to it as the first African country to have large Christian churches. Its ancient history gives it a cultural advantage which may allow it to take a leading part in the mission of God's church in Africa. Over the past years it has also come through fierce persecution with amazing courage and faithfulness. Victory under such fearful suffering always gives Christians a depth of character and spiritual life which can then be shared with others.

The churches of southern Sudan too have suffered severely under the ferocity of Muslim oppression and warfare. They have also witnessed quite a few Muslims being converted through the testimony of Sudanese Christians and also across the border in Libya through Christians working there.

Unfortunately the financial poverty of the African churches has made it difficult for them to send their people as missionaries to other parts of the world. Over the past two hundred years we have developed forms of mission which depend heavily on financial support from the sending churches. This allows the relatively weak European churches to send many missionaries all over the world; likewise the burgeoning economies of East Asia facilitate missionary sending among the Chinese and from Korea and Japan. But the large churches of black Africa with their enormous spiritual wealth remain an untapped source for worldwide mission outside their own continent.

Conclusion

In general it has to be said that in many African churches there is a dearth of quality Bible teaching and theological undergirding. Many churches are

financially poor with the temptation to become unduly dependent on the West. Administrative skills
are also often in short supply. Despite all these weaknesses, the large and fast-growing African church has
so much to contribute to the mission of God's church
worldwide. All of us could benefit from their vitality,
spontaneity of faith, spirituality, joyful humour,
open-hearted relationships and evangelistic zeal.

5

Politics and church growth: what is God doing in Latin America?

'Pray for the evangelical Christians of Latin America in these fearful days of persecution.'

The call to prayer and commitment to share the gospel with Latin America came clearly to us at the theological college at which I was studying back in the late 1950s. In those days the few evangelical Christians of that continent suffered fierce persecution from the very traditional Roman Catholic church. Many pastors were martyred for their faith, churches were often burned down. Bibles were destroyed. The reforming influences of the second Vatican Council had not yet encouraged more enlightened views to spread through the Roman Catholic church.

Many years later a leader of the Bible Society in Bolivia told me of his call to full-time service for Christ. His father and pastor had both gone out to preach in a village, had been met by a Catholic mob and they were stoned to death. At that time he had been just a young boy, but he had determined to

continue the work begun by his father and his pastor.
I was impressed by his open-hearted lack of bitterness which now allowed him a generous warmth in
relations with Roman Catholics.

'You are driving people into the embrace of the
harlot of Babylon', a voice down the telephone accused me. I was in Sao Paulo, Brazil, and had mentioned in a talk some of the new movements in the
Roman Catholic church. But many evangelicals cannot forget the superstitious bigotry of the past and
still see the Roman Catholic church as the unchanging enemy of the gospel. While it remains true that
much of the Catholic church in Latin America still
clings to a corrupt pre-Reformation form of religion,
such attitudes among traditional evangelicals can
result in them becoming a ghetto community with a
sadly negative lack of warm relationships.

If I had been told during my student days that in
the future I would visit and preach in huge Protestant
churches in Latin America, I would have smiled
disbelievingly. What a moving experience to go
therefore to the enormous 'Brazil for Christ' church
in Sao Paulo with its congregation at that time of
thirty-six thousand adults on a Sunday morning. A
thousand red and blue seats on the platform looked
down over the congregation with a row of large
fountains in front illuminated by bright fluorescent
lights. The pastor told me of his problem in persuad-
ing baptism candidates to get out of the cool water
after their baptism. In the hot climate they so enjoyed
the beauty of lying in the pool beneath the huge
cascade fountain!

In Chile too it was moving to attend a morning

service with some sixteen thousand others in the well-known Jotabeche church in Santiago. In other cities too it was exciting to note the large congregations which have developed and are developing over these past years.

Particularly in Brazil and Chile, the mushrooming of Pentecostal churches has transformed the whole religious scene. Around 10–15 per cent of the total population of these two countries is Pentecostal. This has also made it much easier for other evangelical churches to gain a hearing and to grow.

Traditionally the Pentecostals in Latin America have largely flourished among the poor and uneducated. Their pastors are generally men who have earned their position by long years of successful ministry and church planting, not by academic theological training. In fact many of them have little biblical or theological teaching behind them. Indeed large numbers of Pentecostal pastors have very little schooling at all. Sadly their sermons sometimes reflect this and fail to satisfy the needs of the increasingly educated, upwardly mobile younger generation. While it is true that there is a growing number of middle class, more educated Pentecostals throughout Latin America, it still remains the case that large numbers of more educated young people leave their churches. In fact, it is sometimes said that the Pentecostal churches in Latin America are like a bath with both taps on full and the plug out! They are constantly gaining new members through their active street evangelism, but they also lose many. On balance, they win more than they lose, so the bath gets fuller and fuller. And over the years they have gradually begun to adapt to lower middle class people and their appeal is increasingly to those from this background.

The Pentecostal churches are particularly strong in the southern countries of Chile, Argentina and Brazil. In the Andean republics of Peru, Colombia, Ecuador and Bolivia the rather more dour character of the indigenous Indian population influences the whole culture. In this quieter, more stolid society the more extrovert Pentecostal approach holds less attraction and does not gain ground quite so easily. Here the more traditional style of the older evangelical churches relates well. In contrast to both the Andean republics and the lively southern countries, little Paraguay with the strong input of the Guarani people as well as the Spanish remains quietly resistant to all churches. The very sophisticated and urbanized Uruguay also seems to keep all evangelical witness at bay and, generally speaking, the churches find growth hard to attain.

In Central America the influence of the large, culturally dominant United States can never be discounted. This applies also to the life and growth of the church. While Pentecostals and others do flourish too here, we also see considerable movements of very right wing evangelical Christianity which has its base in the Bible belt of the American deep south.

As we said about black Africa, so also with Latin America, it is dangerous to fall into the temptation to generalize. The various countries and peoples vary considerably and this affects the life and growth of the Christian church. This may even be seen within Pentecostalism. When visiting Venezuela I was interested to hear that large numbers of Pentecostal pastors did not claim to have the gift of healing, but all said they had the gift of tongues. This stood in marked contrast with Chile where some Pentecostal pastors did not have the gift of tongues, but all claimed the gift of healing. Is this because at that time Chile lacked widespread medical services and the poor therefore depended on God providing miraculous healing, while Venezuela then had reasonably good health services? God gives his people the gifts which meet the needs of their particular society.

The Roman Catholic church

In the early days of the Spanish and Portuguese conquests of Latin America, the church went hand in hand with the colonial powers. The authorities not only ruled in secular matters, but they also held the spiritual power in their hands. In Paraguay the Jesuit priests functioned as a sort of state government with total authority over the lives of the Indians in their area. In fact the Jesuits even ran their own army and navy to defend their territory from invasion and their trade from foreign ships. While in Paraguay it was the church leaders who also held secular power, in other countries it was the secular governments who ruled also in religious affairs. In both cases the two went together.

Inevitably this situation meant that the church was allied to the rich and powerful. To many it appeared to support the status quo and have little concern pastorally or socially for the poorer strata of society. However, in more recent years a strong reaction to this has changed the character of the Roman Catholic church in the whole continent. Liberation theologians and ordinary priests have emphasized God's desire for justice. They have sided with the poor in the struggle to defeat oppression. Celibate Catholic priests do not have to care for a wife and children, so they find it easier to live sacrificially among the poor in the shanty towns.

Issues of poverty and social justice form the core of the life and thought of the Base Communities, smaller religious group meetings which allow for more discussion, informality and the affirmation of individuals' personal worth.

In the early days of the continent's conquest by the imperial powers, the indigenous peoples were generally forced into baptism, but the new religion of Roman Catholicism merely gave new names to the old divinities. Christianity formed a thin veneer over the earlier tribal religions. Today some church authorities are struggling to overcome this tradition of Christianized paganism by means of teaching through the Base Communities. In the Andean republics of Peru, Bolivia, Ecuador and Colombia, attempts have been made to develop new systems of lay training together with an emphasis on Bible reading. While one applauds these efforts, it has sadly to be noted that traditional religious roots run deep and are not so easily eradicated. Folk religion remains strong – and the Pope is not alone in encouraging it. The Pope on his visits worships particularly at local cult shrines. Many of the church's hierarchy also maintain this emphasis and now even some liberation theologians stress this aspect of the church's life.

The charismatic renewal has also sprung up in Latin American Catholic churches. While it tends to attract the middle classes and therefore to be politically and socially conservative, it has added spiritual warmth to traditional Catholic faith. With some Catholic charismatics a new Christ-centred and biblical approach has evolved, but with others it has merely added a heartfelt vitality to the old forms and beliefs of folk catholicism.

I remember attending a Catholic charismatic meeting in Lima, Peru. I observed that the notices and the church decor were very traditional Catholic, but the prayers and worship were addressed exclusively to the Lord, not to Mary or the saints. After the meeting I asked the leaders about the discrepancy between the notices and the worship itself. They were surprised, for they had not noticed it. Finally one of them said, 'I suppose in charismatic prayer we come to the Father through the Son by the Holy Spirit – and Mary plays no part.' 'Yes, and we are saved by Jesus, not by Mary', added another.

The Holy Spirit was gradually changing their whole theology.

Protestants

As we have already noted, the largest movement in the continent is that of the Pentecostals, but they are not the only churches which show significant growth these days. The charismatic movement has also transformed some of the more traditional churches and brought considerable growth. New charismatic congregations have also developed, particularly in larger cities. Some of the churches founded by interdenominational missions are now large and influential. Thus in Peru, the Peruvian Evangelical Church has a quarter of a million people associated with its congregations and its members have played a significant part even in the world of politics. In the huge land of Brazil with its population of around a hundred and seventy million, a multitude of different Pentecostal and other Protestant churches flourish. In the context of openly spiritistic movements and animistic practices which came with slavery from Africa it is not surprising that more charismatic churches do well. They deal specifically with the demonic backgrounds of those who come to them. The leader of one such church reminded me that western Christians often have an inadequate doctrine of conversion. He rightly pointed out that in conversion we turn not only from sin to Christ and his righteousness; we turn also from the person of Satan to the person of the Lord. In baptism too we not only renounce the works of Satan, but also Satan himself and therefore all previous links with demonic forces. This emphasis makes the Pentecostal churches particularly relevant to the Brazilian situation.

While the Assemblies of God Pentecostals are clearly the largest denomination in Brazil with at least six million members and at least fourteen million people affiliated, the non-charismatic Baptists also flourish.[2] They open a new church somewhere in Brazil every week. They now have over a million and a half people affiliated with them. And they continue to grow.

While the Pentecostals are often rather weak in the content of their teaching, the Baptists have developed a string of Bible schools and strongly emphasize good Bible teaching. Their Bible schools are not only for training future pastors and full-time workers, but also often include night classes for ordinary Christians after work. Living in the middle between other Protestants and the Roman Catholics, there is the Anglican church. In a strange way it is able to relate to all and to serve all with its non-residential Bible courses. These are used widely by a rich variety of churches, as are also their marriage encounter weekends. Although the Anglican church is still relatively small, it is growing quite rapidly in some countries.

During this past decade the Latin American churches have begun to join forces with churches in other continents in the great task of worldwide mission. Particularly from Brazil and Peru a steady stream of missionaries are being sent out to the Muslim world, to Europe and to the Spanish-speaking and Portuguese-speaking lands of Africa. Many new missionary training schools have also evolved. Enthusiastic churches sometimes find it hard to persevere in the support of their missionaries when they are far away from home and this is causing problems. In these early days of mission from Latin America the casualty rate is worrying, but we believe that with time and experience this will improve. God surely has great purposes for his church in Latin America to share their vitality of spiritual life with people around the world.

Under the shadow of the north

Geography should never be forgotten. The countries of Latin America cannot ignore the fact that immediately to their north lies the great economic and spiritual power of the USA. North America dominates the economies of her poorer neighbours to the south. Culturally too the influence of the United States cannot be ignored. Likewise multitudes of missionaries pour south to bring not only the central message of Jesus Christ, but also their particular denominations, doctrinal distinctives, evangelistic methods and finances. This leads to a love-hate relationship in which things American are admired and copied, but in many people there festers some resentment.

In the summer vacations, crowds of young Americans come south to gain experience and serve the Lord while enjoying a short break from their studies. Such short-term mission experience can change their whole outlook on life and in some cases leads on to a commitment to long-term mission work. At the same time, there is a real danger that large numbers of naive and inexperienced youngsters may underline an impression that evangelical churches are pawns of North America, which could cause some resentment among local Christians. This can of course be true in many parts of the world, not just in Latin America.

The dominating wealth of the United States is sometimes seen also in the missionaries whose homes and lifestyles may be very different from those of the people they serve. In one city a mission leader who was struggling with this problem took me on a tour of the city. We went from one mission property to the next in prime sites. At each place he told me the commercial value of the property, which ranged from half a million to several million dollars. No wonder national churches cast covetous eyes on mission finances and sometimes demand the handover of their properties to the local Christians.

Injustice

Our television sets have brought before our eyes the crying needs of the poor in Latin America. I remember visiting a family in a pathetic shack and looking out from their door at the extreme wealth of the business sector just a few hundred yards away. In Lima, Peru, the dreary shanty town areas stretch for mile after mile on the desert sand outside the city. The squalor of some such districts contrasts sharply with the luxurious wealth of the middle classes. The heart-rending fate of the huge numbers of street children in the cities challenges us all to active compassion.

But it is not only the newly urbanized poor who suffer the poverty and indignities of an unjust system. In the countryside and villages the peasants live at the mercy of their landowners. Debt makes them almost slaves to the rich. There often seems no escape from the calamity of poverty and debt when your land and labour are in pawn.

We have seen already that some Roman Catholics have taken up the political cudgels on behalf of the oppressed. Liberation theologians have brought this injustice to the attention of the church worldwide and of the media. Many ordinary priests and nuns actually live in the shanty towns among the poor in order to serve in a very practical way. Protestant theologians and church leaders have also caught the vision of the struggle for justice.

The Pentecostals usually claim that they are apolitical and refuse to get involved in such questions. But in a different way they too have a ministry related to the needs of the poor, for much of their membership comes from such circles. Their emphasis on miraculous healing meets a particular need among people who cannot afford to go to a doctor. Socially, the outcast poor find self-worth and esteem in churches where they are called 'brother', or 'sister', where they can get up and give a testimony and everyone will join in giving glory to God for them and embracing them. In the Pentecostal churches they feel they have importance as people. They don't just sit passively in a pew.

Although most Pentecostal churches avoid all involvement in politics, it sometimes happens that politicians woo their support in elections. In Chile and Brazil particularly, the Pentecostals form such a significant proportion of the electorate that election candidates promise electricity, drains, better water supplies or other benefits for the shanty areas in order to win votes. Dynamic evangelism and resultant church growth do have spin-offs in other areas of life. Of course, it always remains questionable whether politicians will fulfil their promises after the elections!

In non-Pentecostal churches and missions there has been considerable emphasis on social ministries to help the poor. This has not only meant the distribution of food and clothing, medical care and schools, but also the establishing of some cottage industries to give employment and training in work skills. I still use some beautiful leather coasters bought from just such a cottage industry in Lima.

Evangelicals in Peru have played a formative part in the writing of the national constitution and indeed in the attempt to ensure justice and honesty in the political process. In Central America evangelicals have taken the lead in party politics and sometimes have gained high office, but there has been a danger that they have been unduly right-wing in their views and too much under the dominant influence of the United States.

Many people feel that extreme left-wing or right-wing dictatorships have had their day in the continent of Latin America. There seems to be a movement towards more democratic forms of government. The question of justice and greater equality both of wealth and of opportunity still hangs like a cloud over this part of the world. Political, social and economic changes are on the way. What role will the churches play in the process?

Will the Roman Catholic church shake off the overriding influence of superstitious folk religion and allow a renewal of biblical and Christ-centred faith? Will the mushrooming Pentecostals lose their way because of their inadequate Bible teaching? Or will they continue the trend to move increasingly out from among the very poor and uneducated, following the social mobility which allows their young people to move more into the middle classes and gain education? Will the Pentecostals therefore become the majority religion of Latin America and replace the dominance of the Roman Catholics? Will the fast-growing evangelical churches of Central America become the primary religious force of their countries? And will they in South America also continue to grow rapidly and spread into all strata of society with the gospel of Jesus Christ?

Latin America is in flux; it is an exciting continent.

6

Colourful crowds in a continent of differences: God's work in Asia

Christians commonly emphasize how Jesus Christ related to individuals in a very personal way. Less often do we take note of the fact that he also had compassion for the crowds, for example in Matthew 9:36, as he moved among the throngs of people in Israel.

I remember how small I felt standing in the middle of a huge new housing area in Singapore for the first time. Tens of thousands of people swirled round and past me as I looked up at the blocks of flats stretching into the sky. Does Jesus Christ also love the crowded cities of Asia with their population of millions jammed into relatively small areas? Or does he care only for individual families in more spacious suburbs and individuals in rural villages and tribal areas?

Of course Asia does still have tribal groups which need the good news of Christ. Vast numbers of people are scattered in huge rural areas with innumerable villages which hardly find a place on the map. But more and more the multitudes drift into immense cities like Jakarta, Manila, Bangkok, Tokyo, Bombay, Calcutta and many others. When surrounded by the awesome multitudes of Asia we need to remind ourselves that our Lord related, and still relates, to crowds as well as individuals.

Most Europeans fail to appreciate the immense size of Asian populations. China alone has some twelve hundred million people – considerably more than all Africa and Latin America put together. India has a further nine hundred million; Bangladesh over 135 million; Pakistan over 140 million. In East Asia Indonesia now has more than two hundred million – at least as many as Holland, Britain, France and Spain together. Then the little islands of Japan bulge to overflowing with more than 120 million. Asia houses at least half the people for whom Christ died.

Different histories

The silk trade of China and Japan; the spices of Indonesia; the rubber and tin of Malaysia; the romance of the Orient generally – it's no wonder that Europeans were drawn to Asia like bees to honey. The Portuguese conquered large areas, but finally were pushed back to the tiny enclaves of Macao on the coast of China, Goa in India and half the island of Timor in Indonesia. The Danes found their way to India, but did not penetrate beyond that. The Dutch battled with the Portuguese and ended up victorious in Indonesia where they ruled for over three hundred years. The French carved out a niche for themselves in Indo-China – Vietnam, Laos and Cambodia. The Americans arrived late on the scene, defeated the Spanish and enjoyed half a century's colonialism in the Philippines until independence was granted in 1946. The British ruled in the Indian sub-continent and under the genius of Sir Stamford Raffles developed the great city state and port of Singapore. Before that Penang and Malacca in Malaysia ruled the spice trade from the eastern islands of Indonesia. The British also won a toehold into China with the acquisition of Hong Kong, as did Germany in Tsingtao. Perhaps we should note too that for three years the British held power in Indonesia during the Napoleonic wars, leaving a lasting mark on that great country – they still drive on the left and it was under the British that missionary work among Muslims was first permitted there.

The differing colonial backgrounds have left behind a rich variety of economic, educational, political and even cultural systems. Of course not all Asia submitted to foreign domination, for Thailand and Japan remained independent throughout the history of imperialism. Korea never came under western powers, but suffered under Japanese rule from 1910 until the end of the Second World War in 1945.

The various countries of Asia differ not only because of their varied histories in relation to colonialism. They are also very different racially and therefore culturally and religiously.

While the vast bulk of China overhangs all the rest of Asia and sends its people into all lands, the indigenous peoples of the surrounding countries vary considerably. In Korea and Japan, Chinese philosophy and religion have deeply influenced the whole evolution of culture; China has also given them its form of writing. Culturally, however, Japanese, Koreans and Chinese also have marked differences between them. The Thais have intermarried a great deal with Chinese, so that many leading families have at least some Chinese blood in their background. Again the Thais are markedly different from the Chinese, but Chinese influences stand out clearly. During the Vietnam war it was often assumed by western observers that the peoples of Indo-china were fundamentally one. This was far from the truth. While the Lao culture relates closely to the Thai, the much more dynamic Vietnamese are of different stock. Cambodians on the other hand look back with pride to the ancient Khmer kingdom and empire of which they were the centre. The Khmer not only stem from totally different roots from the Lao or Vietnamese, but their historic national pride would not permit them to submit to the domination of another race. Utterly different in every way from all the above peoples are the Malay races of Indonesia, Malaysia and the Philippines. Likewise the sub-continent of India contains a further multitude of different races and peoples. To compare the peoples of Nepal with those of south India is like chalk and cheese.

In religion too we may observe vast differences between the different countries and peoples of Asia. All the major world faiths are strong here. Islam dominates in SE Asia among the Malay peoples and is the official religion of Malaysia, the predominant faith in Indonesia and the distinctive flag of rebellion against the majority Roman Catholic Philippines in the south of that country. Theravada Buddhism, the stricter form of that religion, reigns in Thailand, Laos, Burma and Sri Lanka, while the more accommodating Mahayana Buddhism and Confucianism join hands with Shinto in Japan, with traditional shamanism in Korea and with Taoism among the Chinese. While Nepal is the world's only Hindu kingdom, the majority of Indians also follow the various streams of Hinduism. Bhutan acknowledges Buddhism as its official religion.

Just as the Chinese have migrated all over Asia, so too have the Indians and they have carried with them their Hindu faith. In the melting-pot of Asia mosques rub shoulders uneasily with Hindu and Buddhist temples. And they all vie for the souls of the relatively small tribal groups which still cling to their traditional forms of religion.

This is the variegated context in which the Christian church lives and bears its witness.

The church

Not surprisingly, it is impossible to generalize about the Christian church in Asia. In some countries it is large and strong while in other areas the casual visitor would hardly notice that the church exists. Various expressions of the Christian faith manifest themselves in the different lands of Asia – charismatic, non-charismatic, Anglican, Reformed, Pentecostal, Baptist and a host of other denominations.

1. Strong churches

There are two East Asian countries which possess
large churches apart from the Roman Catholic nation
of the Philippines. In South Korea and Indonesia the
church flourishes and forms a significant part of the
total population – in Korea about 25 per cent and in
Indonesia perhaps about 20 per cent. In Indonesia no
one knows the accurate statistic, for the pressures of
Islam encourage both the government and the
churches to downplay the size and growth of the
Christian church.

Until relatively recently, South Korea's predominant Buddhism held little attraction for large portions
of the population. Korea's rapid development economically and in education outpaced the thinking
and practice of Buddhism, which seemed to many an
irrelevant relic of the past. This meant that it presented little opposition to the rapid spread of the
church in its dynamic witness. In more recent years
however, Buddhism has made considerable strides in
its adjustment to the modern world, often copying the
worship patterns, Sunday schools and university
discussion groups of the church. Today one can even
see well-educated Buddhist monks wearing smart
modern versions of their traditional monks' clothing.

In the early years of mission work among the
Koreans, great emphasis was given to indigenous
structures of self-support, self-government and self-
propagation. The American missionary Nevius pioneered this approach there. The Korean churches
today take it for granted that they are totally independent of any foreign domination. Of course their

size and financial wealth help them to remain free from economic strings manipulated from the West. And the fact that few Koreans read English well prevents British or American Christian literature gaining too much influence.

The Korean churches have developed a thoroughly Korean character which makes it much easier for local people to join them. While the scandal of the cross of Christ may remain, few cultural barriers hinder Koreans from conversion to the Lord and membership of the church. In some ways it is not always easy to see what is genuinely biblical Christian faith and what is just an adaptation of traditional non-Christian Korean ways. For example, western Christians are always deeply impressed by the emphasis there on prayer. The capital city Seoul witnesses even worse traffic jams than usual as people crowd into the early morning prayer meetings. Many pastors will have a couple of days of prayer alone on the 'prayer mountain' before they preach on the Sunday. Korean Christians give the rest of us a tremendous challenge in their practice of heartfelt and believing prayer. But it has to be said that in traditional non-Christian Korean religion it was believed that the longer one prayed, the more likely one was to get the answer. Generally I have little doubt that Christian prayer in Korea stems from a deep trust in the Lord and disciplined dedication to him, but there could just be some whose practice of prayer retains some remnant of the superstitious character of pre-Christian beliefs.

In the early days of Korean Christianity, and particularly under the Japanese occupation, the Christians knew what it was to suffer for their faith. And the church was known to stand for Korean national rights against Japanese Shinto and Buddhist imperialism. The martyrdom of some pastors and other Christians has opened the door for witness today.

I well remember one evening sitting in a restaurant high above the great city of Seoul as darkness fell and the city lights began to twinkle. What an amazing sight! Hundreds of neon crosses stood out in the midst of all the lights. Each of them represented a Reformed church, most of them with large congregations. When talking about Korea, most western Christians think immediately of the huge Pentecostal church founded and led by Paul (or David, as he now calls himself) Yonggi Cho which is the largest church in the world. When visiting I tried to count and reckoned that some 250,000 people attended the various halls in the services that Sunday. This grew to about half a million in the following years, but seems now to have declined considerably. In fact even more Korean Christians throng into the Reformed Presbyterian churches with their total membership of several million. Sadly since about 1990, the various churches of Korea have been losing members, although some congregations continue to grow fast.

The Korean church has been moved by the challenge to world mission. A variety of indigenous missions have sprung up alongside their denominational agencies and Korean missionaries are fanning out into all the world with the good news of Jesus Christ. While there is a particular prayer concern for North Korea, many also have a special interest in the Muslim world. Although some mission training is being done within Korea, much help is needed in this. Their tremendous spiritual power and enthusiasm still often lacks the ability to relate and communicate cross-culturally. Korea is a strongly monocultural society. Few Koreans have the necessary in-depth mission experience to pass on to those in training. Korean mission candidates flood into the theological colleges and Bible schools of the West.

Many Korean churches have little idea how to support their missionaries. Thus some expect a new worker to lead people to Christ and plant churches when they still haven't learned the language. Weekly or even daily telephone calls from the missionary's pastor can put enormous pressure on a young recruit. But they are extremely generous in financial and in prayer support.

In Indonesia too the church has grown enormously. Unlike Korea, however, the Christian church in Indonesia goes back a long way in history. Already in 1611 some 100,000 people had turned to Christ. Since then the gospel has reached out to most of the islands of this huge archipelago. The spread however is uneven. In North Sumatra and Sulawesi whole races have become Christian – for example, the Toba Bataks with some four million people are a wholly Christian group. On the other hand, Islam reigns supreme among many other peoples. So the Aceh people in the far north of Sumatra follow Islamic law with a rock-like adherence to the faith of Islam. Between these two extremes lie the outwardly gentle Javanese, the largest race in Indonesia, some of whom follow Christ while the majority still adhere to Islam.

Most Indonesian Christians belong to the traditional Reformed churches and the Batak Lutherans.

But more recently a multitude of new denominations and movements have come into Indonesia from overseas and yet others have sprung up as new indigenous Indonesian Christian groups. While the external forms of the traditional churches appear quite Dutch because Indonesia was first evangelized by Dutch missions, in fact these forms have taken deep root in Indonesia during the past three hundred years and now appear natural to the Indonesian scene.

The exceedingly rapid growth of the church inevitably produces a need for Bible teaching and training at every level of the church. Many large churches exist outside the cities with little trained leadership and with inadequate teaching. Ordained ministers can sometimes be overwhelmed with their responsibility for several large congregations, so that they churn out baptisms, Lord's Suppers and weddings like sacramental sausage machines. Interestingly, we begin to see a somewhat parallel situation in England with some Anglican ministers having to be responsible for several village churches. Our experience in the Indonesian churches is of a very real hunger for genuine spiritual vitality and for living exposition of the Bible and Christian truth. Christians cry out for training for youth workers, Sunday School teachers, church-planting evangelists and Bible teachers for home groups, rural congregations and baptismal preparation classes. Because of the sacramental and administrative responsibilities of the ministers, much of the teaching and pastoral ministry is in the hands of ordinary church members, elders and deacons.

When presented with the facts of very fast church growth, it is easy to respond with a glad 'Hallelujah'. There is indeed much for which to praise God, but honesty compels us also to face the reality of the weaknesses and needs of the churches. And opposition and even persecution are also increasing with the growing power of Islam. Today there is a real danger too that Muslims are gaining the upper hand in education and the professions as well as in government.

2. *Unresponsive areas*

Asia is a continent of contrasts. The ebullient and mushrooming churches of Korea and Indonesia seem far removed from Japan, Thailand or Bhutan, where the Protestant churches have only a tiny percentage of the population and every new convert to Christ represents a hard-won triumph of grace.

In Japan not only do materialism and the immense pressures of a hard-working society stand against commitment to Christ, but there is further resistance from traditional community values and particularly the practice of ancestor veneration. When a young person adventures beyond conventional boundaries and perhaps becomes a Christian, this may be tolerated, but it is assumed that they will revert to ancestral practices and traditional religion and life when they marry. Backsliding therefore becomes normal for many, so churches remain small.

Many country areas remain unevangelized or strongly resistant to the introduction of the Christian faith, and even large towns and cities will only have a few small churches shining as dim lights in the prevailing darkness. Whole areas of cities may continue without any Christian presence.

Yet the picture of gloom still has a silver lining. Because of their over-population and their economic success, the Japanese spread out from their islands into all the world. Parallel to this, the churches have also developed a worldwide missionary vision. Together with many Koreans and Chinese the Japanese too are sending increasing numbers of missionaries into other countries, including the tough mission work of the Muslim world.

In Thailand, Theravada Buddhism, the stricter form of that religion, mixes with an animistic cult of the spirits to hold the people in bondage. To be Thai is to be Buddhist. The Christian churches can easily be seen as foreign intrusion into Thai life. The apparently easygoing friendly tolerance is hard to penetrate with a message of absolute and unique truth in the one saviour Jesus Christ. Christian witnesses feel like boxers punching a glutinous jelly. It yields politely, gently envelops the intruding fist and quietly returns to its former shape.

Behind the smiling veneer of Thai Buddhism hide very real problems. With the notable exception of the Philippines, Thailand is reckoned to have more inter personal violence than any other Asian country. While Buddhism aims to repress all emotion in its struggle to lose self-awareness, actually it is like a boiling kettle without any outlet for the steam. The peaceful exterior eventually explodes in violence. Sexual immorality and a massive prostitution and AIDS problem bring untold heartache. In more recent years, despite the Pacific Rim economic boom, fearful poverty has increased in some areas. And now Asia's economic problems have caused this poverty to increase still further. Buddhism lacks social solutions to these problems. In spite of some excellent Christian ministry among drug addicts and prostitutes, thus far the Christian churches have not yet gained a name for offering more satisfactory answers to the nation's needs.

With its population of less than a million, Bhutan also lives under the all-prevailing dominance of Buddhism. Here it is a rather superstitious form of lamaistic Buddhism mixed with the pre-Buddhist traditional Bon faith. Bhutan has been extremely cautious about allowing foreigners into their mountain land and it has been hard to penetrate with the message of Christ. A few medical missionaries have been allowed to work there, but they have had to be very cautious about witnessing to Jesus Christ. In all Bhutan there are probably only about a thousand Christians, most of whom are Nepalis rather than Bhutanese. But it is hard to discover in any accurate way how many Christians there are.

Buddhism reigns as the predominant religion also in Mongolia, Burma and Sri Lanka as well as the three countries of former Indo-China.

Under Communism Mongolia was rigidly closed to the Christian faith, but this has left a hungry vacuum. A nationalistic revival of the veneration of their great military leaders from the days of Mongol supremacy has gone hand in hand with the dramatic growth of the Christian churches. As recently as 1992, it was said that only a few hundred Christians struggled to maintain their faith. By 1995 growth had just started and there were about three hundred believers, whereas now these have multiplied to become about ten thousand. And the church continues to grow. Lamaistic Buddhism and Communism have little positive input in the area of morality and Mongolia has a bad reputation for dishonesty and immorality. The Christian churches with their large numbers of very new Christians face the danger of the world's ethical failures infiltrating the life of the church.

For many years Burma too has been a largely closed country with relatively little influence from outside. Economic pressures and political instability have pushed it into a slightly more open stance. Singapore particularly has developed good relations and as a result they have been able to attract quite a few younger church leaders to come to Singapore for training. Singaporean Christian workers have also been able to engage in Christian mission and in regular teaching in the churches. Although more than five per cent of the population of almost fifty million is Christian, these are largely to be found among the large tribal minorities. The bulk of the Burmese Buddhists remain almost untouched by the Christian message. There can be a danger that Christianity relates to tribal rebellion against the Buddhist Burmese in their struggle for autonomy. Such political alignments may underline the impression that 'Buddhist' and 'Burmese' are synonymous terms.

3. Between the extremes

Many Asian countries have neither huge nor minuscule Christian communities, but somewhere between those two extremes. For example, Cambodia begins to fit into that category. Whereas in 1990 it only had some ten small churches, today it has over three hundred – and the number continues to grow.

In Malaysia almost ten per cent of the total population belong to the Christian churches, of which the largest among the Protestants are the tribal churches of East Malaysia (Sarawak and Sabah) together with the Methodists and Anglicans. While about half the population is Malay racially and Muslim religiously, the churches grow rapidly among the Chinese, Indians and tribal peoples. It has been a special privilege to my wife and myself to observe the steady growth of these churches. When we lived in Malaysia back in the 1960s, we knew many churches with only fifty or a hundred members. Most of these would now welcome congregations of two or three hundred active believers. Many have become mature spiritual leaders of high calibre. Financially, as well as biblically and theologically, many of these churches are strong.

Still, much remains to be done. Large numbers of Chinese Buddhists and Indian Hindus still have little opportunity to hear the gospel. Christians often tremble with fear at the thought of sharing their faith with Muslims because it is illegal. Christian books on Islam are banned and Christians have been imprisoned and even tortured for being involved in witness among Malay Muslims. While some Christians remain determined to share their faith freely but wisely with all people, others have been frightened into silence. And yet, it has been encouraging to observe a growing trickle of Malays coming to faith in Jesus through dreams, reading the Bible or through the quiet personal testimony of Christian friends.

An effective social ministry among orphans, children of leprosy patients, drug addicts and other needy groups has been pioneered by Care Malaysia, an indigenous Christian group. Even Muslim officials acknowledge that through prayer their work shows better results than are achieved by parallel non-Christian institutions.

In the Philippines Protestant churches flourish too. Rather over 7.5 per cent of the sixty million population belong to Protestant churches, which at present are growing rapidly. Sadly however the easygoing Philippino culture, reacting with the influx of a wide variety of independent missionaries, has led to an almost ludicrous multiplication of denominations and independent churches. For example, some three hundred Baptist denominations vie with each other and with six Fundamental Baptist denominations – and the constant splitting of Pentecostal churches defies statistical research. Somehow in the midst of this unseemly disunity the Lord still works. As in other Asian countries, God has developed mature spiritual leaders for his church as well as many dynamic spiritually-minded Christians.

In order to escape grinding poverty on the edges of many cities as well as in the rural areas, many Philippinos are working overseas where they can earn relatively large sums of money. Many are serving as maids in the wealthier nations of Asia as well as in the Middle East. Communities of Philippinos are also to be found in America, Australia and in London. In Hong Kong at least 100,000 work largely in menial jobs. These overseas communities are often very open to the gospel and present the church with a challenge and an opportunity. Thus in Seoul, Korea, Philippino congregations have been established in one or two of the larger Korean Reformed churches.

Church and society

The social needs of the continent are enormous and the church responds to this. Churches are involved in ministry among Taiwan's factory workers in their vast blocks of flats resembling the conditions of battery hens. In Hong Kong, Christians have pioneered work among drug addicts and those trapped in industrial sweated labour. Liberating evangelism saves some prostitutes from sexual slavery in Thailand and other countries. As we have seen, Malaysian Care has various residential homes to help ex-prisoners and others in need. Various missions live and work sacrificially in the fearful slums of Indian cities and of Manila. Many missionaries are also involved in social ministries among the poor in Bangladesh. To some extent Asia's evangelism does go hand in hand with social action, but we are only scratching the surface. Particularly in the Indian sub-continent, poverty and injustice stares us shockingly in the face.

China

Over the last few years the world seems to have become aware in a new way of the immense significance of China. Politically it overshadows the rest of

Asia. Economically it represents a vast market place for the world's goods, and international companies are falling over each other in their haste to invest there. While the all-prevailing corruption and inefficiency deters those who possess less financial muscle or political connections, the potential for the future cannot be overestimated. As this giant with one fifth of the world's total population becomes more open to the outside world and takes its rightful place in international relationships, no one will dare overlook its importance.

But China's future remains shrouded in uncertainty. Will it succeed in developing a modern capitalistic economy while maintaining its conservatively communist political structures? Or will the inevitable outside influence which accompanies economic development blow the whole system apart? Will the central government be able to hold this huge country together or will it disintegrate into a mass of semi-autonomous provinces? Will the thirty million Muslims in north west China and the Buddhists of Tibet rebel in civil war or actually secede?

Some years ago I belonged to a rather liberal Christian group for the study of Maoism and communist China. In those days any reference I made to Christians and the church was derided as irrelevant to modern China. Critics thought that only a few old ladies still clung to old-fashioned bourgeois ideas of religion. How wrong they were! When Mao died and more accurate news of the church trickled out from behind the bamboo curtain, we realized that God had kept his people in triumphant and enduring faith. Indeed the churches had multiplied.

As a celebration of the fiftieth anniversary of my wife's liberation from a Japanese prison camp in north China, she and I visited the cities in China where her parents had worked as missionaries, where she had been born, went to school and then was imprisoned. In each place we had the privilege of visiting Christian churches which were packed with people. We were excited to meet church leaders who had come to Christ through my wife's parents or who had been discipled by fellow missionaries of those pre-revolutionary days. It was a great joy to hear good biblical preaching in registered churches as well as knowing that the unregistered churches stand clearly for true Christ-centred teaching. In each church we attended it was desperately difficult to find a seat, and often there were crowds standing in the extreme cold outside in the courtyard.

We can only guess how many Christians there are now in China. Some cite figures as high as a hundred million or even more, while others estimate a mere thirty million. Between the two extremes many China-watchers consider about fifty million a reasonable guess. In any case we know that the relatively small churches of 1948 have mushroomed despite the years of horrendous persecution and militant atheism. In those days many Christian leaders were killed and others suffered fearfully for twenty long years in labour camps.

Throughout the dark years of persecution the government allowed the official church to remain in compromised political subservience. In this way the authorities presented a picture of freedom to visiting dignitaries from overseas. Today increasing

numbers flock into their services and many new
official churches have been opened, but restrictions
still remain and in some areas even persecution
continues. But the greatest growth has come in the
independent house churches. It is reckoned that
probably about 80 per cent of China's Christians
belong to these unregistered house churches; the
remaining 20 per cent attend the open churches of
the Council of Christians in China, but most are
nevertheless quite biblical in faith.

For British readers we need to point out that these
'house churches' have little in common with what
used to be called 'House Churches' in Britain, for the
Chinese independent churches may often be strongly
non-charismatic. This varies from area to area and
from church to church – some are strongly charismatic while others have a different tradition. But all
these congregations strongly reject any compromise
with the state and refuse to allow government inter-
ference in their choice of leaders, the content of their
preaching or in the forms of their meetings. As a
result they have suffered particularly ferocious persecution. Martyrdom and prison have threatened
them for years.

Before the tragic events of Tiananmen Square life
had become somewhat easier for the churches, but
then the government cracked down again and Christians began to suffer once more. Gradually now the
thumbscrews are being eased in some areas, but presumably the nation's leaders are well aware that Eastern Europe's revolutions found their focal point in the
church. They therefore feel the need to keep a watch-
ful eye on the church lest the same should happen in

China. The government rightly fears the social and economic chaos which has afflicted the former Soviet Union. They know too that the Chinese empire could easily disintegrate just as the Soviet Union has broken into a variety of independent republics.

What happens in the immense land of China cannot but overflow and influence other areas of Asia. The miracle of the church's enduring faith and growth in China should encourage us all. When China really opens fully to the outside world, its church will play a major role in mission to other countries. Meanwhile the door for expatriate workers has opened into China and increasing numbers of overseas Chinese Christians are being used of God to help teach and train the churches. Westerners too are visiting China to share their medical expertise, while many others live there full-time as teachers of English or other subjects. Their witness in China's current spiritual vacuum can be significant and it may encourage the national churches. Good standards of language learning will prove essential if they are really to communicate effectively. After years of isolation from the church worldwide and of persecution the church's greatest need is for good Bible teaching. Expatriate Christians can teach those local believers who become their friends; and they in turn can pass on that teaching in their churches. Chinese society is changing rapidly these days and developing fast, so the church will also need to move with the times. New and younger leadership has to be trained. Churches require good biblical exposition and an apologetic ministry which relates to current issues and debates.

But foreigners will need to be humble and patient, not rushing into China with our own plans and ideas. We need to work sensitively in co-operation with local Christian leaders and under their direction. We must resist all temptation to introduce our particular spiritual or theological lines which will divide the church. Gradually we may be sufficiently accepted to be able to help with the Bible teaching, training and good literature production which are much needed.

The Indian Sub-continent

In the imperial days of British India the whole sub-continent belonged together as one country. Then with independence it divided into Muslim Pakistan and the secular, but largely Hindu India. Later in 1971 after a bitter war East Pakistan declared its independence as the nation of Bangladesh. Although Pakistan and Bangladesh both contain huge populations of over a hundred million each, India still retains the great mass of land and people. With over nine hundred million people India is more heavily populated than all Africa or Latin America. In many ways it has to be said that India is more like a continent than just a country.

In the formation of the Muslim state of Pakistan the leaders of Islam were declaring that to be a true Muslim one needs to be in a Muslim state and under Muslim law. Inevitably this leaves considerable question marks in the minds of India's large Muslim population of more than 110 million. Are they second-class Muslims just because they have not moved to Pakistan or Bangladesh? Their position in India remains somewhat ambivalent – and this has been accentuated by the militant violence of some Hindu extremists with communal fighting.

Although India is largely Hindu, Christians also form a considerable minority with about four per cent of the total population. These are concentrated in the far north-east tribal areas of Nagaland and Mizoram together with the large traditional churches of Kerala. Kerala has been the centre of the Old Mar Thoma churches which claim to have been founded by the apostle Thomas and which can certainly trace their history back to around the fifth century. Belonging to the Orthodox family of churches, they abound in ritual but also often exhibit very real spiritual life. Owing to the history of the Mar Thoma churches, Christians in Kerala belong almost entirely either to the higher castes or to the lowest – Hinduism rules supreme in the middle castes.

While the southern states of India hold a reasonable number of Christians, the more northern parts are dominated by Hinduism with relatively few churches. Thus the ecumenical united Church of North India is very much smaller than the Church of South India. Although various denominations have united in the CNI and CSI, the individual congregations usually maintain their denominational backgrounds with fierce tenacity.

Just as the overall population of India is mainly living in the villages despite the huge pressures of mass urbanization, so among Christians the majority come from the lower scheduled caste. Officially the Indian constitution and laws stand firmly for equality of all citizens and thus against traditional caste distinctions; in practice caste is observed strongly by almost all Indians. While Christians oppose caste distinctions with their inevitable discrimination and injustice, it still proves very difficult to plant new cross-caste churches or to remove the practice of caste in existing congregations.

As might be expected in a church of some 36 million people, we find a rich variety of active Christian movements. Under the umbrella of the Evangelical Fellowship of India come a range of radio and cassette ministries, the Evangelical Literature Fellowship with various affiliated literature ministries and bookshops, the widespread evangelistic and training work of Operation Mobilization, the influential student ministry of the Union of Evangelical Students of India, youth work through Youth For Christ and others, theological extension programmes under TAFTEE. Up and down the country are located some 150 Bible schools, seminaries and other training establishments. The Bible Society flourishes with many Bible translation projects as well as the task of wide distribution of the Bible. The Jesus film is already shown in a variety of Indian languages with considerable fruitfulness.

On the social front India also abounds in organizations which concentrate on the tragic needs of the poor. The Emmanuel Hospital Association has several prestigious hospitals and an influential medical ministry. Others stress work in the fearful slums around the vast cities of Bombay, Delhi, Calcutta and other urban centres. Street children, AIDS victims, leprosy sufferers and other needy groups are the goal of various Christian ministries.

For some years it has been hard for expatriates to obtain visas for work in India as missionaries, but this has by no means inhibited the life and growth of the Christian church. Indian churches are strong and they also have various indigenous missions for the evangelization of their own peoples. Stephen Gaukroger in his *Why Bother with Mission?*[3] claims that India has the largest number of missionaries of any non-western nation. It is always difficult to determine precisely who is a missionary, but he says India has 8,905. *Operation World* records that India already had more than eleven thousand missionaries in 1992, representing 198 agencies. The largest is the India Evangelical Team, but perhaps the most significant groups are the Friends Missionary Prayer Band and the Indian Evangelical Mission. The majority of Indian mission workers are located in the north of the country and particularly among the minority tribes.

Just as China has large numbers of its people living all over the world, so too Indians can be found in every continent. They have brought their Hindu, Sikh and Muslim faiths with them, challenging the local populations to cross-cultural mission. The largest concentrations of Indians are found in Nepal, Malaysia and Sri Lanka, but there are also considerable communities in America, Canada and Britain. In Trinidad, Fiji and Suriname they form a significant proportion of the total population; in Mauritius Indians are in the majority.

a) Bangladesh and Pakistan

With natural disasters and fearful poverty haunting the nation, Bangladesh has been the recipient of considerable relief work both from Christians and non-Christians. Bangladesh has also captured the attention of British people because of the large numbers of its people who have come to live in England. Many of these are from the province of Sylhet, a strongly Muslim area of Bangladesh. As a result, Christians in Britain think of Bangladesh as quite fundamentalist in its practice of Islam, but in fact the majority of Bangladeshis are relatively easygoing in their religion. Nevertheless, the relative minority of more fundamentalist Muslims exert an influence beyond what their numbers should warrant. As a result, Bangladesh moved from being a secular state into an official Muslim state in 1988.

Less than half of one per cent of the population of Bangladesh professes to be Christian. Most of these come from Hindu or tribal religious backgrounds with only a few thousand issuing from the Muslim majority communities. And still today most Christian witness concentrates on the Hindu and tribal minorities with relatively little attention being given to Muslims.

In visiting Bangladesh, however, I have been encouraged to note how Muslims are turning to Jesus Christ. Where Christians determine to make relationships and witness among Muslims, there will usually be some who come to repentance and new life in Christ.

This has been observed particularly among certain groups of contexualised ex-Muslim Christians, but it is happening also through the everyday personal witness of Christians in Dacca and elsewhere.

Unlike India, there is a dearth of Bible schools and theological colleges. A handful of denominations run their own small schools, there are a couple of inter denominational Bible schools, but otherwise the church depends on untrained leadership or people who have studied a little in an extension course or some part-time classes. The already existing training establishments are therefore of particular importance for the future of the Bangladesh church. In the context of so much paternalistic relief and aid work, it is vital that good well-trained leaders be prepared. Otherwise there is a real danger that the church could remain largely dependent on overseas assistance.

While Dacca, the capital city of Bangladesh, is thronged by some seven million inhabitants, Karachi in Pakistan tops the sixteen million mark. In Dacca it is rare to see many women in the streets except early in the morning and after work when long queues of women make their way together to and from work. In Karachi larger numbers of women may be seen shopping or walking from place to place. And yet Islam is stronger in Pakistan than in Bangladesh and one senses the dominant influence of Islam in Pakistan's daily life.

In Pakistan the church claims a larger percentage of the population than in Bangladesh. Perhaps as many as three per cent are Christian, although some claim a figure as high as five per cent. The largest denominations are the quite traditional Anglicans and Presbyterians which face the danger of second-generation nominalism with an accompanying spiritual lifelessness.

Struggling to bring a new vitality to traditional Christians as well as to share the gospel with non-Christians are such ministries as the Pakistan

Fellowship of Evangelical Students and the Pakistani movement for theological education by extension.

In the far north west of Pakistan large numbers of Afghan refugees swell the local population of border tribes. Various Christian and non-Christian aid bodies seek to minister to the broken bodies and traumatized lives of these refugees in Peshawar and the surrounding area. Large refugee camps can be seen on both sides of the Afghan border. The wild scenery may fascinate the tourist, but life is hard for those who live there in primitive camps. And the heat can be fierce with temperatures up to 50°C.

It is from the Pakistan side of the border that Christian radio broadcasts are prepared for beaming into Afghanistan. When these were first aired, no letters at all came from Afghanistan in response. Islam seemed rock-like in its resistance to the Christian faith. But in the last couple of years quite large numbers of letters have come with requests for New Testaments or other literature. Muslims are now asking questions, wanting to know what Christians believe and whether there is a viable option to Islam. That whole area of north-west Pakistan and Afghanistan have been the seat of extreme fundamentalist Islam, but some are beginning to see from the Afghanistan experience that its fruits are not good.

b) Nepal

For many years this Hindu kingdom was closed to foreigners and the Christian faith was sternly outlawed. Although the country opened to outsiders in

1951, it was still not at all easy to gain access. Christian workers who were called to mission in Nepal lived and served across the border in N. India. I remember the excitement when some of my contemporaries first crossed the border and actually lived in their promised land.

Even in those days, however, the gospel was beginning to make an impact on Nepalis. Some were converted in India. Nepali Gurkha soldiers came to faith in Christ while serving in the British Army. Already in the 1960s when serving in Malaysia we had a group of Christian Gurkhas in our home each week. There was a large Gurkha garrison in our town of Kluang and several came to faith in Christ there during our time in Malaysia. We always admired their courageous witness in the face of fierce opposition from their officers as well as from other non-commissioned soldiers.

Operation World quotes statistics to demonstrate the amazing growth of the church since 1951. It says that in 1960 there were 25 baptized believers in Nepal; in 1985 this had grown to 25,000; in 1991 at least 50,000. And now we have little idea of the numbers, for the churches are multiplying at an incalculable rate. New churches are springing up even in quite remote areas. Partly because of the mountainous terrain and lack of roads or other forms of communication, it has proved difficult to keep the churches in unity together. Various coordinating bodies have been formed, but none has really functioned effectively.

The main expatriate input has come from the United Mission to Nepal with some four hundred members, the International Nepal Fellowship with over a hundred and the beginnings of student work through the International Fellowship of Evangelical Students. The UMN and INF have played a major role in introducing good medical facilities in cooperation with the government. They have also had a significant influence ecologically through the UMN's reforestation programmes. UMN also has responsibility for a large hydroelectric scheme which will bring considerable development to the country.

Many Indian Christians have also come to work in Nepal and they play an important part in the teaching of the many young churches as well as having a vital witness among non-Christians.

In our opening chapter we noted how righteousness, peace and joy in the Holy Spirit are the marks of the kingdom of God. It is very evident in Nepal that the coming of the Christian faith has brought believers to a new desire for holy living both personally and in interpersonal relationships. And when one visits Nepali churches the joy of the Lord is striking. Of course there are still grave weaknesses in each of these areas, but a marked change from their pre-Christian days is evident. God's Holy Spirit is at work not only in bringing rapid numerical growth to his church, but also in changing the lives of new Christians.

The kingdom of Nepal is beginning to become the kingdom of our Lord Jesus!

Conclusion

This chapter on Asia is much longer than those on other parts of the world. We could have divided it, dedicating a whole chapter to China and the Indian sub-continent on their own. But the very length of the chapter illustrates again the reality that Asia houses the great bulk of the world's population. China alone holds as many people as the whole world of Islam.

Perhaps too the length of the chapter reflects the fact that the author has lived and worked in Asia, so it has a special place in his heart.

Nevertheless, these few sample situations provide only a taste of the multifaceted diversity of Asia. With its vast populations, dynamic economic development, high levels of education and the strengths which come from a long history of sophisticated philosophy and culture, Asia is well placed to become the next great centre of the Christian faith.

7

The biggest church of them all: God's work in North America

Skyscrapers dominated the skyline on a brightly coloured postcard produced by a Christian mission in the United States. Beneath the array of imposing buildings stood the slogan, 'Every little village dreams of becoming a major city'. My thoughts went back to the Hertfordshire village where we live. Did people there dream of Stanstead Abbotts one day becoming a huge city with all its wealth, traffic, crowds of people and towering office blocks? Our village might consider this more of a nightmare than a dream.

But of course it remains true that success will produce growth. Churches which demonstrate the vital life of Christ will attract new people into their congregations. If people come to life in Christ and are brought into the church, then inevitably that church will become larger. This very obvious principle applies equally to mission societies. If they attract new recruits and do not lose members through attrition, they cannot remain small. Growth in numbers does indicate an inner vitality which draws new members into fellowship and keeps them. The growth of the New Testament church provides a clear example of this. As Europeans we must be careful not to despise the American dream of dynamic growth. The slogan 'small is beautiful' may merely justify stagnation and lack of vision.

What image does the expression 'American Christianity' conjure up in the average European's mind? We shall probably think immediately of the scandals of television evangelists. We are all aware of the dangers of huge wealth, media glamour and considerable popular influence. Right back in Old Testament times, God continually warned his people of the dangerous temptations of power, sex and money. Christians today still need to heed those warnings and our leaders must work within structures of close personal accountability. European television enjoyed the unseemly pictures of American television evangelists confessing their sexual sins with public tears. The superficial glamour of their tinsel world placed dark question marks over their repentance and indeed over the sincerity of their gospel preaching. Such suspicions apply equally to the huge American drive-in churches, crystal cathedrals and slickly professional church services where beautifully trained choirs produce their songs like automatic machines dispensing cans of Pepsi Cola. Elsewhere glib promises of miraculous healing attract gullible crowds.

But is all this really representative of American Christianity? Or have we allowed the media to shape our impressions of the American church? Of course such aberrations do form one aspect of the whole, but

there is much more. It has been said that American
history has produced an emphasis on freedom and
democracy. The founding fathers escaped from British persecution which demanded monochrome con-
formity. Then the pioneering movement westwards
across the vast unexplored continent led to a spirit of
independence and adventurous initiative. This encourages everything and everybody to develop to
their full potential. It is true that sin and heresy can
also flourish, so that we are shocked by gross immorality among some well-known Christian personalities and by the mushrooming of every imaginable
sect and heresy. But we must not ignore the parallel
reality of good things which also multiply and flourish. Success stories abound in American churches
and missions. Again and again we are regaled with
tales of American churches which have grown from
nothing to massive congregations with thousands of
active members in just a very few years. New dynamic missions spring up to evangelize the world
and to reach out to areas and peoples where the
gospel was largely unknown. Major movements like
Operation Mobilization, Youth with a Mission and
Frontiers all stem from American roots. It is hardly
imaginable that such ministries could have been pioneered in Europe! Influential new thinking on mission produces renewed vision and relevant strategies
for local evangelism, church leadership and structures, and worldwide mission. They can inspire and
mobilize large numbers of Christians in a way which
we in Europe find very difficult.

In a previous visit to a Central Asian city in a
previously closed area of the world I found some

thirty-five Christian workers. It did not surprise me to discover that the great majority of them came from the United States. They have a pioneering dynamic which inspires them to find ways to push open new doors for mission. It is true that our American friends sometimes trample over national sensitivities with a naive lack of wisdom. They are sometimes even worse than the British at learning languages and adjusting to other cultures, but their warm-hearted confidence and friendliness often compensate for such failures. While European missionaries may demonstrate wisdom and cultural sensitivity in their work under the direction of local Christian leadership, the pioneering spirit of American missionaries gets the job done. We proudly feel they have much to learn from us, but we desperately need some of their enthusiasm, zeal and drive. British Christians particularly need to imbibe some of the positive optimism exhibited by many American Christians; we tend to view things with such critical negativism that we dampen initiative and positive expectation.

The church in North America represents a vast array of large denominations and movements, independent churches and para-church organizations. Such a huge and variegated church defies any brief descriptions which can only over-simplify in their generalizations. It is estimated that well over 40 per cent of the total population of the United States regularly attend church. This means that the American church contains about a hundred million Christians, whereas British churches attract a mere four million. According to Patrick Johnstone's *Operation World* the Southern Baptist Convention alone has well over twenty million people and all the Baptist denominations together attract around forty million. Such statistics show how tiny European churches actually are, and compel us to realize the influence which the American churches wield in the Christian church worldwide.

European Christians may feel somewhat uncomfortable with the rather traditional right-wing Christian culture of the 'Bible belt' in the southern states of the USA. We may be critical of the fact that most such churches have little concern for racial or economic justice, so that wealthy middle-class white churches stand in marked contrast to shabby black churches nearby. In some cases Christianity may represent a cultural package rather than a dynamic commitment to the living Christ. Many may adhere to an established set of doctrines with an attendant list of 'dos' and 'don'ts' which can replace a real study and knowledge of the Bible. Despite all the weaknesses of Bible belt Christianity, these churches do lobby for moral decency in society, fighting against the inroads of pornography, media violence and widespread abortion. They also give sacrificially for the work of mission worldwide and send large numbers of missionaries overseas. European Christians could learn something from them.

In former years when the pioneer American settlers began to move west across the continent, the more traditional churches tended to remain comfortably in their east-coast buildings. Sadly, they frequently lacked the vision to follow the rugged pioneers as they opened up the huge new territories across America to the Pacific Ocean. As a result

Christians gathered in free and independent churches in the central and western states. While in Europe it is the mainline denominations which still represent the majority of the church-going population, in America free and independent churches attract large numbers. In Europe the ecumenical World Council of Churches is influential, but in America less than half the churches owe any allegiance to it. In Europe, evangelical Christians form only a minority of the total church, while in America they are the great majority.

As we have already noted, the church in America contains a rich variety of movements. There is not only a multitude of denominations, but also churches among many different races. Immigrants of many nations from all over the world have come to the United States in search of a new life and together they have built a society of incredible diversity. Millions of Hispanics, blacks, Koreans, Chinese and Italians rub shoulders with the largest and most influential Jewish community in the world. And there are also considerable communities of people from all sorts of other races, tribes and peoples. Missionaries working in a tribe in Thailand or elsewhere may find more people from their tribe in California than in their country of origin. A whole variety of ethnic churches has emerged, such as Jewish messianic synagogues, Chinese, Japanese and Korean churches. Black churches in America have begun to send their people back to West Africa as missionaries, although they quickly discover that their black American culture differs radically from that of West Africa. This is equally true of Korean,

Chinese and Japanese Americans wishing to return to their mother countries. In the search for our roots we sometimes forget that very different plants have grown in the soil of another country. Nevertheless these ethnic churches are developing a significant new potential for worldwide Christian mission.

A tradition has evolved in North America for many young people to study for a year or two in a Bible school after graduating from high school. As a result huge Bible schools have trained a multitude of Christians for service in their local churches or for wider mission. Crowds of these young students will travel overseas for their vacations for a short spell of work with a mission, particularly in the neighbouring continent of Latin America. It may be debatable just how much use such immature short-term workers may be for the churches and in evangelism abroad, but there can be no doubt that a proportion catch the vision for overseas mission and will return long-term. In the American churches too the Bible schools provide a reservoir of workers with a good basic knowledge of their faith and the Bible. The churches' all-age Sunday schools benefit significantly from this. While the Bible schools may attract thousands of students onto their immense campuses, the graduate study seminaries provide more exacting studies for relatively smaller numbers. Many of the seminary students have their sights set on full-time ministry. As in most other countries, these training establishments have significant influence on the character of American church life and theology. Some of them have adventurous programmes of study which provide a thorough but open-hearted training. Others have a rigid and doctrinaire approach which forces students into a particular theological line and does not permit any divergence from what is taught. American seminaries and Bible schools range from a very high quality to quite a low level of academic studies, although sometimes even the schools of lesser reputation may still grace their graduates with BA and MA degrees.

The independent and democratic character of American life also influences the American approach to education and the media. Whereas in Britain, Christians are urged to get involved in secular television and radio in order to introduce a more Christian influence into these very strategic means of communication, in America the emphasis lies rather on forming specific Christian stations. Likewise British Christians have always attended normal secular schools, colleges and universities. In America Christian educational establishments are common. Of course this American pattern shields young people from the harmful influences of a secular or even anti-Christian environment. They may grow up with clean and wholesome attitudes which are uncontaminated by non-Christian culture. British parents may feel somewhat jealous of this. But on the other hand such young people can find it hard to relate to the non-Christian world around them. Life in a holy ghetto does not equip us for effective personal witness in the non-Christian world. Christian educational establishments also rob secular schools of the salt and light which Christian students should contribute.

Because of their particular history many American Christians have developed some rather rigid doctrinal distinctives. Few British Christians know whether their view of Christ's second coming is pre-millennial, post-millennial or a-millennial. This de-bate hardly touches our churches. But in the United States a sound evangelical faith often goes hand in hand with a premillennial position. As a result pre-millennialism has frequently been considered a cen-tral tenet of the faith. Likewise many will consider that membership of a church which belongs to the World Council of Churches in Geneva disqualifies you as a true believer. This can cause problems over-seas in mission. For example the leading Bible schools and seminaries in some countries were founded by such American missionaries. They have therefore adopted a premillennial and anti-ecumeni-cal stance and so will not welcome any teachers who hold a different position. This may mean that Euro-peans will not be able to join their staffs even if they are in other ways well qualified for the job.

For many years American evangelicals were largely opposed to the charismatic renewal. Today this is changing in some circles. John Wimber's Vine-yard churches and some other independent charis-matic churches have flourished and grown. They have begun to have a wider influence, but still it remains true that the charismatic renewal dances only at the edges of mainstream evangelical life in America.

Overseas mission

Statistics on mission are notoriously unreliable, but it is sometimes claimed that some 70 per cent of all

foreign missionaries come from the United States.
Many large mission conventions like the huge Inter-
Varsity conferences at Urbana challenge the youth of
America to mission. Certainly the strength of Christianity in North America gives birth to a confident
and dynamic vision for mission worldwide. As we
have already noted, American missionaries do not
have a good reputation for cultural sensitivity, language learning or willingness to work under existing
Christian leadership locally, but their drive and initiative compensate for this. European missionaries
often concentrate on development ministries and on
pastoral, Bible teaching work within national
churches. It is true that the Third World desperately
needs medical, agricultural and other developmental assistance. Likewise overseas churches may excel
in other areas of their life, but they are frequently
weak in Bible teaching. While the Europeans edify
the church and assist society in these ways, the
Americans have more of a vision for evangelism and
church planting. Of course these are over-simplified
generalizations with many notable exceptions, but
one cannot but notice around the world the number
of new churches and even whole denominations
which have come into being through American missions. They may be accused of separatism and di-
visiveness, building their own kingdoms, but
through them men and women are finding new life
and salvation in Christ.

As a lecturer in mission it impresses me how
many of the new ideas about mission stem from
American sources. While I dislike much of the
simplistic jargon which accompanies such new

thinking, I have to admit that it seems to capture people's attention and it becomes central to current communication on mission. It is also American mission thinkers who are often in the forefront of re-thinking evangelistic strategy as we face the challenging task of mission today.

For example, it has been Americans who have led the way concerning 'homogeneous units' in which 'messianic synagogues' and 'messianic mosques' may gather together people of a particular culture into churches which are specially suited to their back-grounds. Objections are raised concerning exclusivism, but clearly there is a need for all of us to hear the gospel communicated with our language and cultural forms. We all need Bible teaching which relates to our particular questions and problems. Worship is more likely to engage our hearts and minds if it uses forms with which we feel comfortable. It is obviously help-ful if non-Christians of each race and cultural group-ing can see that Christianity relates to them. Thus many people assume that you cannot be a Jew and a Christian at the same time. The existence of specifi-cally Jewish churches gives the lie to such objections. Jewish Christians may therefore be very grateful to our American friends who have pioneered thinking and practice in this area of contextualization.

More recently the slogan 'unreached peoples' has been coined. Much debate has raged on the exact meaning of a 'people'. Some have limited it to an ethnic group which has its own language and cul-ture. Others have tried to widen it to every social grouping which is conscious of its particular identity – so, for example, London taxi-drivers might be a 'people'; pensioners might be another 'people'. These definitions are related to the Great Commission in Matthew 28 where we are told to make disciples of all nations/peoples. But actually the word used by Matthew merely means the gentiles. He is showing how the task of mission is now not only to preach to Jews, but also to all gentiles of every background everywhere.

But the call to go to the 'unreached peoples' has communicated widely and God is using it to mobilize many young people for the task of world mission. Through it traditional missionary societies are being galvanized into new vision to reach out beyond the churches and areas in which they were active before.

But the 'unreached peoples movement' also has some grave weaknesses. First, its statistics are often gravely inaccurate. Secondly, it can seem patronizing. When a western or Korean church 'adopts' an unreached people, do they ever ask that people whether they want to be adopted? Then too it stresses pioneer evangelism and church planting to the detriment of other forms of mission. Of course we need pioneer evangelism, but mission also includes the work of edifying and training national churches. It also should involve us in other areas of social need.

In the unreached peoples movement we note the tendency that young Christians feel it is they who have to do the work, whereas the task of evangelism is usually better achieved by local Christians. It panders to our pride that we feel we are God's chosen instruments. This may lead to missionaries bypassing the national churches.

American mission thinkers have not only led the way in practical mission theory, but also in communication. They have a brilliant way of simplifying complex ideas and expressing them in neat packages with clear diagrams and a host of supporting statistics. However, the resulting over-simplification does not really describe the depths and complexities of people, religions or situations. Often the statistics may be untrue, more the result of guesswork than accuracy. For example, as we have already seen, we have no possible means of knowing how many Christians there are in China, but the statistics of this one huge country inevitably affect the overall figures for the world. Recently the ludicrous statistic has been quoted and requoted that in AD 100 there were twelve unreached people groups per congregation of believers! The definition of a 'people group' is far from clear and we really do not know how many such groups existed in those days. And we have absolutely no possible means of knowing how many Christian congregations there were in AD 100 – for example, had the apostle Thomas actually reached India and, if so, how many churches did he plant there? And how many churches did Mark plant in Egypt? We just don't know.

But having laughed at such ridiculous statistics, we have to admit that they really communicate and convey a clear and moving message – much more so than the carefully accurate, philosophically defined words which emanate from us in Europe! They grab the attention, make a definite impression and influence Christian involvement around the world.

American Christians also take the lead in matters of organization. The postman recently delivered a circular from an American organization informing us of the Christian conferences and consultations we would do well to attend in the coming year if we wanted to keep abreast of mission today. About forty of these were considered of fundamental importance. As they were located in various cities all over the world, you would have to travel widely. Are some people becoming professional conference-goers? The proliferation of such conferences and consultations has gained epidemic proportions. Nevertheless it is good in moderation. Christian workers find it helpful to meet one another, to learn from each other and form links of cooperation. Professional consultations on mission among Muslims or other such pressing issues can prove most rewarding. Major conferences like the international Lausanne get-togethers form a stimulus to worldwide mission. And when one attends consultations or conferences of this nature, it is quickly evident that it is Americans who have the finances and organizational skills to run them. This can lead to an unfortunate American domination of international meetings, but without their leadership the whole exercise would probably flounder.

The American missionary movement has developed considerably the potential of short-term workers and of so-called 'tent-makers'. In contemporary western culture young people find it hard to commit themselves long-term to a particular ministry. We live in an age of rapid and frequent change. Few people today remain in one job for more than a few years. So too in mission, candidates may think in terms of four or five years, although their knowledge

of the local language and culture will inevitably
never attain a satisfactory level. They will also not
succeed in forming deep personal relationships in
cultures where friendships develop slowly. On the
other hand short-term workers can fill the many gaps
in mission work. They will also learn something from
their experience of the church overseas which they
can bring back to enrich their home churches.

'Tent-makers' go overseas in their professions, but
with the aim of sharing their Christian faith with
local people and playing what part they can in the
life of a local church. Such workers will meet with
many local people whom the full-time missionary
may not be able to reach. They may also be able to
help in the church if English is spoken locally. Otherwise they can be isolated through lack of time to learn
the language adequately. In some countries 'tent-
makers' are purposely trying to stay for a good number of years in order to get right into local society and
make deeper personal relationships. Some take the
time to learn the local language either in the country
itself or before going there. This is particularly true
of those who go to areas of the world which do not
allow Christian workers, for example the Muslim
world. It is exciting these days to observe the large
numbers of such 'tent-makers' from America and
elsewhere in 'closed' countries.

As Europeans we are often suspicious of anything
which comes from America and yet we usually
follow in their footsteps. The influence of the huge
Christian church in North America cannot be
overestimated. With the immense size and diversity
of the American Christian movement there are

inevitably some weaknesses and failures, but we Europeans need to note rather the great strengths from which we have so much to learn.

Canada

When talking of North America it is tempting to concentrate on the United States, but the Canadians would hardly forgive us if we failed to include them too. With the exception of Russia this is the largest country in the world, but much of its landmass lies in the remote frozen north. Despite its size it has less than thirty million people.

In the United States, Fuller Theological Seminary in Pasadena, California, with its affiliated school of world mission has had a worldwide influence. In Canada, Regent Theological Seminary in Vancouver has also drawn large numbers of students from around the world and given them an excellent academic training. With a more traditional evangelical character, Prairie Bible Institute has trained and sent out a multitude of Canadian and American missionaries. The Canadian church has a worthy tradition of developing a variety of good quality seminaries and Bible schools.

The steady decline of Protestant churches in Canada during this century has mirrored what has happened to the churches in Europe. They have struggled with the same problems of liberal theology undermining the credibility of the churches and robbing them of a positive message. As in Europe, moral issues have dogged the Canadian churches too. And the Roman Catholic church suffers from the same problem of non-attendance at mass as the Catholic church in southern Europe.

But there is also a more encouraging parallel with Europe. Pentecostal and charismatic churches have shown considerable growth, as have also some more definitely evangelical non-charismatic churches. Perhaps the greatest growth has been seen in the Christian and Missionary Alliance churches.

During the 1980s an interesting new movement evolved among the French-speaking people of Quebec. Considerable numbers of disillusioned Roman Catholics came into a life-giving faith in Jesus Christ and began in a new way to base their faith on the Bible as their ultimate authority. They did not feel happy to join existing Protestant churches which were culturally alien to them, so formed a chain of new ex-Catholic congregations and Bible study groups. Since the 1980s the growth of this movement of God seems to have slowed down considerably, but the potential remains for further growth.

8

A fast-changing world – God's work in Western Europe

Large question marks hang over the future of Western Europe. What political and economic implications do these next years have as the countries of the continent draw more closely into union? What will this mean for each particular country and region? In drawing closer together to each other will the European nations isolate themselves from the United States, the British Commonwealth and the rest of the world? Will a federated Europe rival the economies of the Pacific Rim? Or will closer union lead to such tensions that the European countries will clash fiercely against each other and pull radically apart? And how will future developments affect education, culture and religion?

Computers and information technology increasingly determine the course of life today. Those of us who remain computer-illiterate seem quaintly traditional in the fast-moving contemporary world. Pen-pushing clerks have vanished from our banks and offices, computerized telephones have ousted human operators, our supermarket purchases brush past the eagle eye of the computer at the checkout point. Gone are the old days of more intimate personal encounters. Only the few remaining village stores still know their customers personally, call you by name and pause to chat. One day I dared to address the checkout lady at a supermarket and commented on how busy she was that day. She replied with amazement, 'Thank you. You are the first person to talk to me this morning.' The affluence of our fast-moving modern society can easily rob us of our personal relationships. Western society is suffering from this depersonalization. And many people feel they no longer have meaning or value.

Rapid and constant change characterize modern life. No longer do we remain faithful to one particular brand of petrol for our car; a small incentive sends us rushing to open an account with a different bank or building society; mid-career changes of profession give renewed job satisfaction, while others face the shock of redundancy. Change prevents boredom, the great enemy of today's western world. We see these cultural developments affecting Christians too. Many feel free to move from church to church to satisfy their own tastes in worship, teaching or styles of leadership.

Marriage too comes under threat not only through this desire for change, but also from the pressures of work. The ambition to succeed and to get money or the fear of losing one's job drives people to work long hours and so have little time with their marriage partner and children. Television drowns out all meaningful communication and marriages can drift apart. The lack of real happiness at home then pushes people to stay longer at work, spend the evenings in the pub or escape through some sporting hobby. Thus a vicious circle develops which frequently leads to divorce and misery. A few years ago I did a small survey among men who were fishing in our local river. Over 90 per cent declared that they came fishing in order to gain 'a bit of peace from the wife and kids'.

Sadly these social problems in Europe undermine the life of the church too. We know from the New Testament that the sins of the world easily infiltrate the church, so we are not surprised. But it presents us with a challenge. European churches are becoming more aware of their need to give their members the real sense of community which our society lacks. Fellowship and relationships have become vitally important. Faced with the insecurities of modern life and its consequent personal heartaches, Christians in Europe today strongly emphasize pastoral counselling, marriage enrichment and the care of the elderly. Theological colleges and Bible schools now train students pastorally, realizing that preparation for Christian ministry does not just mean filling students' heads with theology. The danger in Europe at present may be that we are swinging the pendulum too far. Theology and biblical study have sometimes been edged out of church life in favour of pastoral sensitivity and subjective spirituality.

But the need for skilled pastoral care remains vital. In recent statistical surveys it has been shown that 40 per cent of British people will at some stage suffer from some form of psychological or mental trouble which is serious enough to require medical care. Thirty three per cent of all tertiary education college and university students will see a doctor for such emotional concerns.

The growth of existentialist post-modernism has meant that the younger generations are searching for spirituality. In competition with New Age and eastern religions our churches are called upon to demonstrate a genuine vitality of spirituality. The traditional Christian emphasis on truth and biblical teaching will have to be presented in the context of a cultural opposition to rational argument and objective facts. In the depersonalized loneliness of contemporary society we must evidence a spiritual life which works out in warm personal relationships.

In the post-modern age we need as Christians to address openly and publicly the concerns which people now consider of vital importance. Sexist language and male domination in the church will militate against effective evangelism today. Biblical teaching on the relationship of Christian faith to ecological concerns will attract young people. It is of course a basic Christian truth that God not only created the whole world, but he has also so designed his creation that the righteousness or sin of his people has direct implications for the welfare of our natural environment. When Israel sins, the land suffers judgment; when righteousness prevails, milk and honey flow in peace.

Catholic and Protestant

Traditionally western Europe has been divided into two overall groupings, the largely Protestant nations in the north, and the Roman Catholic countries in the south. Today this division has begun to diminish. The whole continent is equally afflicted with materialistic secularism and unbelief. The traditional forms of Catholicism and Protestantism have failed to relate effectively to our changing societies, leaving the mass of our populations dissatisfied. This has led to a widespread disaffection with the church, although a spiritual hunger remains. And with the growth of post-modernism this concern for spiritual things is deepening. Dynamic and culturally relevant churches still attract good congregations. But many people still seek spiritual reality and satisfaction through eastern mysticism, traditional paganism or the occult.

The Roman Catholic church

Protestants sometimes think of the Catholic church as a monolithic unity, but actually a variety of currents flow through the church and produce different movements. For simplicity's sake we may define four main streams within contemporary Catholicism.

1. The traditional

The present Pope, supported by the Curia in the Vatican, strongly upholds the traditions of Catholic theology, spirituality and ethics. This section of the church does not change in its beliefs about the infallibility of the Pope, the role of Mary and the saints, the old sacramental doctrines, celibacy of the priesthood, and opposition to all birth control. When the Pope visits a foreign country, he always makes a point of praying at the main local shrine to Mary and of reaffirming traditional Catholic teachings. Protestants have to realize the strength of such folk religion in traditional Catholic communities. Those of us who live in countries where the Roman Catholic church is a minority can easily be misled. We may enjoy considerable fellowship with Catholics who follow more biblical and charismatic trends. As a result we may not be aware of the very superstitious and biblically unacceptable forms of Catholicism which usually predominate in traditionally Catholic countries.

2. *Liberal and political*

In reaction against traditionalism, and often influenced both by Protestant thought and by Liberation Theology, some today embrace radical liberal theology and biblical criticism. Sadly they fail to see the consequences of such destructive approaches in the history of the Protestant churches, where the spread of liberalism and the undermining of faith in the reliability of the Bible gradually emptied our churches.

Many within the Catholic church have also reacted against the power of a hierarchical church which inevitably aligned itself with state authorities and the rich. Latin American liberation theology has played a significant part in moving the church to side more with the poor and oppressed. Social and political involvement in support of the powerless has become an integral part of contemporary Catholic thought. While most of us would rejoice in this development, we have also to note the danger that liberation of the oppressed can replace rather than supplement the work of Christ in his death for our sin. Salvation from oppression in this world can become more important than eternal life and reconciliation with God himself.

While some High Church Protestants have converted to the Roman Catholic church because of their opposition to the ordination of women in Anglican and various other Protestant denominations, it is also true that many Roman Catholics are unhappy with their church's rigid opposition to the ordination of women, the marriage of clergy, birth control etc. So there is movement in both directions.

3. Biblical renewal

In Reformation days Catholic bonfires destroyed Bibles and their translators. How things have changed! Today Catholics are strongly encouraged to read their Bibles and the church plays an active part in distributing the Scriptures. Inevitably the reading of the Bible can influence people's beliefs. Although the church seeks to encourage its people to interpret the Bible in line with the official church teaching, the written word of God still speaks powerfully. For example, one priest has openly declared that he will no longer teach about purgatory, for he does not find this dogma in the Bible. Through Bible reading the centrality of Jesus Christ is becoming a new reality for some.

4. Charismatic renewal

A sophisticated young teacher told me enthusiastically how she had been filled with the Spirit and so had a new warmth of love and faith. Eventually it became clear however that Jesus remained quite secondary to her, for her spiritual experience had merely reinforced her love for the Virgin Mary. In contrast to this, the Vicar General of a Scandinavian Catholic church told me how his charismatic experience had made Jesus and the Bible central to his whole faith. Sometimes the charismatic renewal merely warms and enlivens traditional Catholic religion; in other cases the Holy Spirit is doing his work of glorifying Christ and opening the Scriptures.

Protestant churches

For simplicity's sake we may divide Protestantism into three categories – state or mainline churches, free churches and newer charismatic churches. Increasingly these three groupings relate and work together more closely in opposition to the inroads of secular atheism, eastern religions, New Age and the occult.

1. Mainline churches

Throughout western Europe these Reformation churches face twin dangers: liberalism, which undermines the very foundations of the Christian faith, and rationalistic traditionalism which stifles vitality in the dreary cotton wool of irrelevance. Legalistic adherence to rigid and outdated structures inhibit the mobilization of the laity and the growth of the church. In the struggle to maintain tradition, many resist all attempts to make the life and worship of the church contemporary. In pastoral love and graciousness we may submit to the wishes of older members who dislike change, but in so doing we alienate the unchurched and the younger generation. Boredom is the one thing young people today will not tolerate.

But these mainline churches remain in the centre of our nations' bloodstreams. In many ways they stand at the heart of the national life. If people face problems or sense a hunger for God, they will naturally look to the state church for pastoral or spiritual help. At the crucial times of birth, marriage, sickness and death the church is expected to play a significant role. This gives such churches a particular responsibility and opportunity.

Happily we are witnessing today new movements of life in these traditional churches. A new freedom and a spirit of adventure have transformed some congregations which are therefore growing again after years of decline. In Norway evangelical theology gained precedence over liberalism in the last century, and the Lutheran state church remained spiritually strong until secularism opened the door to liberalism more recently. But now revival movements are again renewing the church. In Britain steady decline has characterized the Anglican church for years, but now the downward slope of the graph has begun to turn upwards. The much heralded decade of evangelism in the 1990s has encouraged the Anglican church to be ready for growth, but often rigid structures and deeply entrenched clericalism inhibit the potential.

Throughout western Europe it is the mainline churches which hold the key to any possibility of a general turning back to Christ throughout the nation. These churches are central to national cultures, and they can influence the whole world-view of their peoples. However, most of them still remain with little life or vision except in little pockets of spiritual dynamic. We need to pray much for them.

2. Free churches

Strangely the so-called 'free' churches sometimes face a particular danger of cultural stagnation and conservatism. They face the temptation to mistake cultural forms for biblical forms essential to the life of the Spirit. On the other hand they have often remained faithful to Scripture and Christ when the mainline churches have surrendered to the onslaughts of liberalism. With their freer organizational structures comes the opportunity to relate flexibly to modern society without compromising their faith. While the evangelical churches in Germany and Switzerland often fail to change with the times despite their members' warm love for the Lord and his word, in Holland and increasingly in Britain signs of adventurous life are emerging. Sadly, in southern Europe the ghetto mentality of evangelicals in formerly strongly Catholic or Greek Orthodox societies still prevents the churches from effective witness in increasingly secular surroundings. They often appear to outsiders as culturally irrelevant sects which have been imported from America or northern Europe.

3. Newer charismatic churches

The main growth of the church in Europe in recent years has come from the charismatic renewal and the new churches which have emerged as a result of it.

That is not to say that growth has not also taken place elsewhere, for we have already observed for example that evangelical Anglican churches have also flourished. Yet it is principally the charismatic renewal which has introduced a new life and vitality into many traditional churches. New songs have multiplied with the renewed emphasis on worship. Many Christians have found liberty and a freshness of faith as they have come into the experience of spiritual gifts.

The advent of the charismatic movement has unfortunately brought some traumas as well as rich blessing. It has often divided churches, so that disunity and bitterness have pushed love to one side. Happily, we see a growing desire now to quash that spirit of rivalry and replace it with harmonious cooperation. Perhaps the decade of evangelism has further cemented this growing desire to work together.

In many cities in Europe, as well as in other continents, the annual March for Jesus has brought together large numbers of Christians from different churches. They unite in a prayerful demonstration to show that the church is alive and relevant to contemporary society. So often we all meet in our separate little churches and the world around us hardly notices that we are of significance. Yet far more people go to church in Britain on Sundays than attend professional football matches, but somehow we fail to impress people with the church as a popular mass movement. The thousands of vibrant Christians who join the March for Jesus around the world, help to rectify this situation.

The charismatic emphasis on direct prophetic

words from God has sometimes led to an unfortunate weakness in theology and careful biblical exegesis, but this is not always the case and some are coming back to a greater desire for sound biblical teaching and preaching. Likewise the early overemphasis on miraculous healing has given way more and more to an awareness that in God's grace, suffering of all sorts may not always be clearly demonic. More recently 'spiritual warfare' has come into prominence and we still often lack a careful biblical approach on this subject. But in many parts of Europe, and indeed more widely throughout the world, the charismatic movement has really helped the church to face the realities of Satan, demonic activity and the occult. These are now so common in our societies that we cannot ignore these issues in our preaching and teaching.

The largest Bible School in Europe is in Uppsala, Sweden. The Word of Life Bible School attracts hundreds of young people with its dynamic and youthful enthusiasm. Sadly, its teaching strongly emphasizes that God blesses people of faith with material prosperity. They stress that all sickness comes from Satan and Christians ought not to suffer. They therefore deduce that Job only suffered as he did because of his lack of trust in the Lord. Prosperity teaching of this sort works like a magnet, drawing young people to a triumphalistic confidence in their faith. It fits the materialism of western Europeans as well as white South Africans, among whom such teaching is also strong. It gains ground like a forest fire in Eastern Europe where many people covet the wealth of the capitalistic West. It is easy for them to equate atheism with poverty and Christian faith with material wealth and prosperity.

While the charismatic renewal has often now settled with greater maturity into the mainstream of European Christianity, new, more radical movements have broken out. All over Europe the Toronto blessing has struck like lightning to bring a new encounter with the living God, a new sense of the power of God – and also yet more disagreement and division. If such movements bring people to a more fervent love for Jesus Christ and a new passion for worldwide mission, we shall rejoice. It remains too early to be able to judge their long-term effects, but we shall know them by their ongoing fruit.

Emanating from the large Anglican church, Holy Trinity in Brompton, London, the Alpha courses have spread like wildfire not only through Britain but also in other European countries. Although these courses stem from a very upper-class church with immense human resources, they are being widely used in churches of all sorts. Through them God is bringing new people into life in Christ, as well as renewing many spiritually stagnant traditional church people.

The charismatic movement tends to stress dynamic spiritual life rather than truth of doctrine, personal relationships of love in the Spirit rather than traditional church life in which religion remained a private matter between God and the individual. This would not only seem more in tune with original first century patterns of Christian life, but it is also well fitted to relate to new movements of postmodernism.

4. Ethnic churches

Throughout western Europe ethnic minorities abound. People from many nations have flooded into our countries and settled here. Tragically they have not generally found a warm welcome even from the Christian churches. As a result they have largely formed separate communities where they can feel secure in their own cultures.

This has also affected the development of the church. Our European churches have not known how to adapt to other races and cultures. Their worship forms have been very western in style and their teaching and preaching patterns have not related to African and Asian ways of looking at the Bible or theology. The churches' preaching has often been quite unrelated to the questions which face those who have come out from other religions or whose cultures differ from ours. Some have tried to settle into our white churches, but have found themselves alienated by the cool welcome. For example, Afro-Caribbean blacks came to Britain with strong church connections in Anglican and Methodist traditions. When they felt themselves rejected by the white British churches, they formed their own black churches which have mainly been Pentecostal.

In the larger cities of western Europe a proliferation of ethnic churches has developed. For example, in London there are several Korean and Chinese churches as well as the many black churches. Then one can find Japanese, Jewish, Spanish, Portuguese, Arab, West African, Norwegian, Finnish, Indonesian, South Asian, Greek, Russian ...

These ethnic churches flourish, meeting the particular needs of their own particular people. But they have little or no input into the British churches which would benefit so much from their vision and life. And the ethnic churches would also have something to gain from the maturity and biblical teaching of the British churches. In the New Testament it is said that no member of Christ's body should dare to say to another member, 'we have no need of you'. All of us have much to learn from each other and we shall be impoverished if we receive nothing from other churches of different racial and cultural backgrounds.

Issues in the church

1. *Pluralism*

Christians in the West face the fact of other religions on their doorsteps. Muslims, Sikhs, Hindus, Buddhists and Jews have flocked to our cities. In our schools children receive teaching about other faiths and learn to appreciate them. In fact, the schools' attitude to other faiths is often more positive than what is said about Christianity. More and more Christians begin to question the uniqueness of Christ and the Christian faith. The question of the Christian approach to other religions burns hotly.[4] This issue has also emerged as the front-runner objection to the gospel among non-Christians. 'What's so special about Jesus?', they ask, 'Why Jesus rather than Krishna or Mohammed?'

The focus of this issue has sometimes centred on the question of whether Jews should be evangelized. As we have seen, some Christians feel that Jews have their own way to God through the Old Testament covenants, while Jesus came to open the door for gentiles. They maintain then that Jews do not need the gospel of Jesus Christ. They also affirm that in the light of the church's history of persecution of Jews, Christians have no right to share their faith with Jews. It is then pointed out that if Jews can find salvation without Jesus, so can monotheistic Muslims and indeed people of other religions also. In fact, all evangelism becomes an unwanted arrogance.

In the pluralism debate Christians are often considered intolerant and proud if they insist on the need to preach the gospel to others. Tolerance has been heavily stressed, but it is in fact only tolerance of those who share the same cotton-wool tolerance. Such people demonstrate an extreme intolerance towards those whom they consider to be intolerant!

Biblical Christians need to address these issues seriously. Christ gives his disciples the clear mandate to evangelize all peoples of every background.

2. *Oppression*

No longer are European Christians merely interested in personal salvation and our spiritual relationship with God. The claims of the oppressed have touched our hearts and entered our theological thinking. We have begun to see God's concern for the widow, the orphan, the poor and the oppressed. This applies to those who suffer socio-political injustice, and also to the victims of racial discrimination. While Christians are themselves not innocent of racial prejudice we want to stand with our ethnic minorities in our own continent and with people everywhere who suffer discrimination.

As Christians we have just begun to be aware too of the question of sexism. No longer can we get away with sexist language, using 'man' for humanity etc. The role of women in society and in the church has become a hot potato. But we have hardly yet come to grips with the question of 'speciesism', the human domination over and misuse of non-human species and of our environment. Although New Age is often credited with being the leaders in issues of gender and the environment, actually Christians too have played a significant role in these battles.

3. Moral issues

With the decline of Christianity in most western European societies, immorality has become more obvious around us. The sins of the world have a way of influencing the church too. Debate rages therefore on abortion, homosexuality, premarital sex, divorce, excessive use of alcohol and drugs. The younger generation in the church cries out for help and teaching on these topics, but often older church leaders have become either unthinkingly legalistic or unbiblically permissive. Sometimes these issues go hand in hand with occult practices which have also become very common in our societies today.

We need to recover the biblical emphasis that worship of the holy God must always be accompanied by holy living. God demands that his followers should reflect in their lives the beauty and purity of his own nature, so that the world might see the glory of God in and through the lives of his people. Christian ethics are not based on a list of divine taboos, but on the character and nature of God himself. We are to be holy as he is holy. This is the fundamental condition for the worship of the all-holy God.

Evangelism

In the 1960s the churches faced their steady decline by dreaming nostalgically of revival returning to our countries as it had in previous centuries. In the 1970s we saw the need to revitalize the life of the church as a prerequisite for any future evangelism. In the 1980s more churches began to move out in evangelism, but often their forms of worship and church life militated against effective outreach. In the 1990s we have started to see actual growth in more lively churches.

In the past we have fitted our structures around feeding fish in our church aquariums rather than becoming 'fishers of men'. Training for the ministry has also concentrated on preparing church leaders for a pastoral and teaching ministry among the faithful, not for leading the church in out-going evangelistic mission. But in Europe today we face the new situation in which the church only represents a small minority of the overall population. The call to mission in our own countries stares us in the face.

As we have seen, the people around us struggle with overwhelming problems – loneliness, marriage breakdown, interpersonal tensions, deep insecurities etc. As Christians we believe that the gospel of Jesus Christ is indeed good news in every context of need. As Jesus has declared in the Sermon on the Mount, our righteousness as his disciples cannot be hidden, but needs to shine out visibly into the world's darkness. Such open witness may well result in the suffering of persecution, but as Christians we find fellowship with Christ as we walk in his footsteps, for he is the suffering servant.

In the second half of the 1990s churches in Europe have begun to emphasize and practise the missionary ministry of church planting. Although church planting always formed a basic part of the ministry of missionaries overseas, it was a forgotten art in Europe until recently.

Church planting varies in its methods. Some churches are starting new congregations within their original building, but often these new congregations are reaching a different sort of person – perhaps the church was attracting largely older people, but now they have also a service designed for a younger clientèle. Other churches are separating off twenty or thirty of their gifted members to start a new church in another area, making sure that between them the team of church planters have a variety of gifts for ministry. New churches are also being planted as a result of small home groups or childrens' meetings which gradually grow into something bigger.

Different methods may be used, but what is important is that new churches are being started in villages and urban areas which until now have remained without an active church presence.

So in this decade of evangelism we face the challenge of bringing our countries back to the gospel of Christ. It is encouraging to note some media interest in Christian things – are we becoming more newsworthy in this post-modern age? Realizing the immense influence of the media, it is vital that biblical Christians gain a hearing not only in the newspapers, magazines and local as well as national radio, but also and particularly on television.

In our renewed concern for evangelism and church planting in Europe we are confronted with the danger of insularity. We may become so caught up in our passion for winning our own countries that we lose our missionary vision for the rest of the world. Jesus himself taught that it is actually more blessed to give than just to receive. This truth relates well to our situation. If we fail to give sacrificially to other areas of mission, we shall experience how God will not bless us in our home mission. The churches overseas may lack many things in which we may be able to share with them, but they do have considerable experience in evangelism and church planting. Many Christians overseas have assumed that church planting is a normal part of the Christian life. They have much to contribute to us in this decade. In giving to them we shall ourselves receive.

Conclusion

Western Europe has experienced long years of spiritual decline which has half emptied our churches. Today relatively few merely traditional church-goers remain. The church has generally become slimmer but fitter, although a heritage of discouraged lack of expectation often permeates the life of the church. Nevertheless an increasing dynamic can be observed among Christians. At the same time a growing disillusionment with secular materialism and the rat race is gaining ground. While some look for answers in the dark world of the occult and even witchcraft, others seek solace and peace in eastern religions and New Age. But an open door presents itself also to churches which have confidence in their message of Christ, and witness to the gospel with cultural relevance and obvious spirituality. Post-modernism is opening peoples' hearts to what is truly spiritual.

As we face the new millennium it seems that the church in Britain and parts of Scandinavia may be well placed to take advantage of the open doors God has given us. Holland too has many churches which are in a good position to grow. In some other countries a narrow conservatism and even a ghetto mentality may sadly stifle effective outreach and hinder the possibilities of church growth. And some areas of Europe are more open to the gospel than others. Southern Europe's increasing anticlericalism makes these countries difficult for the gospel. Belgium's hard materialism dampens all evangelistic outreach. On the other hand Germany used to be dark spiritually after the horrors of Nazism and the Holocaust, but as the past moves more into history, Germans of the younger generations have become much more responsive to the gospel of Christ.

May God's word and Holy Spirit impart true life to us all in our various churches and send us out in effective evangelism.

9

The death of Marxism in the year of revolutions – God at work in Eastern Europe

Future students will all learn about 1989 as a turning point in world history. While 1917 saw the beginning of the Marxist experiment, 1989 witnessed the final collapse of a dead system. Many of us watched our TV screens and saw the immense crowds thronging the cities of Eastern Europe and toppling the apparently impregnable might of Communist regimes. The outward appearance of power hid the rotten core of economic, social, spiritual and moral breakdown. Eastern Europe has set out on a new path which has not been an easy one and many pitfalls still lie ahead. Europe's years of division have come to an end.

Through television we have learned of the fearful economic chaos which Marxism has brought to the countries of eastern Europe. Thus Russians joke about the nationality of Adam and Eve. Were they English, French or . . . ? No, they were certainly Russian. Only Russians could share one apple between two people, have nothing but fig leaves for clothes and still call it paradise. We have seen pictures of empty shelves in the shops. But did our television convey adequately the vital role played by the churches in these revolutions? In almost every situation the church formed the foundation for the new movements of freedom, peace and truth.

When visiting Prague just after the Velvet Revolution, I was told of the importance of truth. They joked that the main Russian newspaper *Pravda* (which means 'truth') contains no truth, while the other newspaper *Izvestia* ('news') has no news. Many observed that only the church could be trusted to speak truth. They also talked of the mass demonstrations in Wenceslas Square and the damp November evening when two secret policemen were discovered filming the crowds. They were dragged in front of the people. Would they be lynched, their limbs torn from their bodies in mass hatred and revenge? Just at that moment, a church minister climbed the platform and called on the crowds to kneel on the wet streets to pray the Lord's Prayer – 'Forgive us our trespasses as we forgive them that trespass against us'. Many told me how that moment turned their revolution from bitter revenge to forgiving love and kindness. These lovely Christian characteristics formed the foundation of the revolution and the new society which needed to be developed. But the heritage of the past, and human failure, have meant that this has proved far from easy.

This is the challenge to the Christian church. Atheistic communism has left a spiritual vacuum as its legacy. Will the Christian church fill the emptiness with the practical and spiritual truth of Jesus Christ, or will western materialism draw the multitudes of Eastern Europe to dedicate their lives to Mammon? After years of drab poverty the glitter of western capitalism and the consumer society beckons almost irresistibly. From the fringes of Christianity extreme 'prosperity' teaching draws people with its simplistic promises that faith in Christ will always bring material blessings and will save from suffering and sickness. The vacuum is also being filled by eastern religious sects and New Age movements. Yoga and Zen meditation have flooded into these countries.

What then of the church? Western Christians dare not criticize our brothers and sisters who have suffered for Christ, endured long decades of fierce persecution and anti-religious propaganda, but have won through. Who would have thought twenty years ago that the mighty power of Communism would crumble so quickly and that the poor, oppressed churches would triumph? We cannot but praise God for his faithfulness and grace – and we salute the courage and enduring faithfulness of our sisters and brothers. Now we need to pray for them as they face the new challenges in situations of freedom. In many ways they are ill-prepared for this and, humanly speaking, they could easily lose the battle of the future.

For many years in most east European situations it has been impossible to invite non-Christians to church services. Evangelism took place on a one-to-one basis. Then after commitment to Christ new Christians would dare to join their brothers and sisters in more public worship. This has meant that church services were aimed at definitely committed

Christians who were willing to pay the price of active persecution. Going to church often meant losing one's job, even being sent to prison. One Russian church elder told me that most of his members had spent time in prison for their faith. Worship therefore was serious, not intended at all to entertain. If this emphasis on seriousness without joyful communication is continued, they face dangers. They may lose the younger generation and also fail to attract into the church those who at present are looking for an ideology by which to live. Western churches have much to learn about serious faith, absolute commitment to Christ and a willingness to suffer for him. But perhaps we may also have something humbly to contribute in our more joyful and lively forms of worship and teaching.

The church needs to fill the ideological vacuum, but then also to demonstrate how Christian faith gives a love and delight in Christ which satisfies every aspect of our personalities. This came home to me when I was in Prague just after the 1989 revolution. A middle-aged man came to the church where I was speaking and informed me that he had never before visited a church. He then told me that until recently he had been professor of atheism in the prestigious local university, but was now out of a job as atheism had become unacceptable. He was asking about Christianity – can an intelligent professor believe in Christianity? What does it mean for practical living if one becomes a Christian? If Czechs became Christian, what would that mean for the whole political development of the country? Or for the nation's economics? Or for agriculture? Or the medical world? Or for education?

In the past, Marxist atheism had been the all-embracing philosophy which undergirded everything – politics, art, education etc. Every society needs an adequate ideology, for otherwise it will disintegrate into meaningless chaos. I began not only to try to answer his questions, but also to ask myself about modern western society.

The east European situation compels us to look again at the Bible, our message and how we present it.

1. The biblical message

The unchanging message of God's coming to the world in the person of Jesus Christ, his death for our sins, his resurrection to bring us new life and his final second coming in glory to bring his kingdom to fullness – all that remains the same whether it is preached in Eastern Europe or anywhere else. But it may have different applications and emphases. For example, after years of persecution and pressure some church leaders as well as many ordinary Christians have compromised with the Marxist state authorities. For them the cross of Christ signifies an open door to forgiveness. For others who have suffered for their faith, the cross demonstrates a God who knows what it means to suffer, and the resurrection may show that the sometimes traumatic after-effects of long years of persecution can yield in Christ to a new life of joyful victory. And the cross also calls them to forgive those who were weaker than themselves and compromised. As God forgives, so we should forgive.

In recent visits to the former Soviet Union and Eastern Europe, I have been impressed by the vital relevance of Paul's cosmic understanding of God's saving work in Christ. In Colossians 1:15-20 the repeated emphasis on 'all' underlines the reality that Christ's redeeming purposes extend not only to all peoples everywhere, but also to the whole creation. In the ecological disaster of Eastern Europe, it is highly relevant to point out that in the Bible we are intimately linked to our environment. Human sin brings tragedy to nature, godly obedience to the Lord leads to harmony in nature. Christians in Eastern Europe face the challenge to work for the restoration of this harmony. They can also look forward to the climax of history when God will not only redeem us and there will be a new humanity, but he will also redeem all things and creation will be renewed. No longer will sin corrupt us and our societies, nor will pollution poison the earth – even the desert that was the Aral Sea will have new life in Christ. The disastrous tragedy of Chernobyl and the other Ukrainian nuclear power stations will be no more; no more babies will be born with horrendous deformities, for the air and the land will again be pure. What a message of good news! Unfortunately it still seems a distant dream.

In this post-Marxist age Jesus Christ and his church bring good news. In a society where in the past no one trusted anyone else, the biblical emphasis on loving relationships brings a smile to deadpan faces. Christ's humility as the servant can renew society as people begin again to learn the values of courtesy, gracious humility and service of others.

In our churches in the West, little emphasis is given to biblical teaching on truth; but after years of Marxist propaganda and fear, the central importance of truth takes on new meaning. Christians have much to contribute as they live and speak truth. All these great realities of the gospel of Christ can flow freely when Jesus Christ becomes the centre of our lives both as individuals and in society. In the spiritual vacuum which results from the death of Marxist atheism, we have to ask again whether the church is prepared to live and preach such a relevant gospel. If it does not, will western secular materialism replace Marxist dialectical materialism? Or will a spiritual drug-injection of eastern religious mysticism, or the blandishment of crass western-style 'prosperity' teaching fill the void? Or will these countries just return in disillusionment to a slightly less autocratic form of Marxism?

After the collapse of the Communist states many dreamed of a better and freer society. In practice, freedom has allowed the Mafia to gain power, extremes of wealth and poverty have developed, everything has become available in the shops, but people can't afford them. Crime, violence and immorality have flourished. But there is freedom and the bullying attitudes of officials have been reduced. People now smile in public.

Post-communist freedom is a heady mixture of good and evil.

2. Communication

For several decades it was extremely dangerous to evangelize openly in Eastern Europe, but now Christians are learning to reach out publicly. In Moscow airport I heard a group of Pentecostals singing and preaching in the entrance hall. While admiring their zeal and courage, I also sensed that their patterns of communication failed to attract people. In some parts of Central Asia Christians now preach and witness in the parks, but one wonders how far their methods are attuned to their non-Christian hearers. As yet, such public witness is relatively new, so hopefully Christians will quickly learn to adopt new approaches which will appeal to non-Christians. Perhaps some western Christians may be able with humble sensitivity to suggest the use of drama, more contemporary music or even symbolic dance. But such forms must not just be taken over from western backgrounds; they will need to be adjusted for different backgrounds. If they are introduced too quickly or without cultural sensitivity, local people may reject them like the body can reject an alien organ transplant. But gently and gradually we may be able to encourage local Christians to appreciate the vital importance of active evangelistic witness and to experiment in culturally suited forms.

A group of young Czech Christian leaders were discussing how best to work in the new post-revolution situation of religious freedom. One suggested that we need more Christian literature to teach and train Christians in biblical truth and mission. Then they talked about literature which could be used in evangelism to answer the questions which are commonly asked by people with an atheistic Marxist background. One young man objected, claiming that under Communism, anything printed was a lie, so people would assume that Christian literature was also propagandist untruth. Much debate ensued, but finally all agreed that we need more literature, but that it must be so written that readers would clearly see that it is not just propaganda.

The influence of the Communist period remains in other ways too. For example, a pastor recently told me that it took some four years in a ministry before people would really trust him. Long years under a régime where spying on each other was encouraged leaves a heritage of mistrust. Gradually the Holy Spirit is giving Christians such a love for one another that a greater openness can follow.

Soon after the Communist régimes collapsed, I saw a lay-training course which some western Christians were using in Eastern Europe, but which had been produced by Christians in the West. It started with the question, 'Who is Jesus?' and then gave the short, simple answer, 'Jesus is God'. Three biblical verses followed to prove the point. The style resembled Communist propaganda and made it unusable in Eastern Europe without considerable change.

It remains true however that Eastern Europe desperately needs a wider range of Christian literature. There are so few commentaries to help pastors and other Christians to study and teach the Bible. Gradually more western commentaries are being translated, but this means that we impose a western understanding of Scripture on these churches. They really need to write their own books. This applies not only to commentaries, but to all sorts of books. They lack basic works on Christian doctrine and teaching to help people appreciate the riches of their faith and be able to discern between true and unbalanced emphases. This is vitally important because all sorts of sects and Christian extremes have flooded into Eastern Europe. Devotional books, books on practical Christian living, books for children and young people, Sunday school teaching aids, help for Christians to understand Islam and eastern religions in such a way that they can witness effectively – so much is needed. In the West, we have such a wealth of Christian literature of all sorts; Eastern Europe still lacks this.

Often when we think of mission in Eastern Europe, we refer only to western Christians working there. In recent years, I have been excited to share in training Russian, Ukrainian, Moldovan and other missionaries who were taking the gospel of Christ, at great personal cost, to the far corners of the former Soviet Union. Such workers hold the key to the task of mission in these lands.

Traditional churches

As evangelicals in Western Europe our attention goes all too easily to parallel churches in the East to the exclusion of more traditional churches. It remains true however that the majority of Christians still belong to the old mainline denominations. The Roman Catholic and Orthodox Churches claim the allegiance of millions, as does the Lutheran Church in the eastern part of Germany. In the 1989 revolutions Christians from these Churches often led the freedom movements, and the early demonstrations and rallies found their focus in a church building belonging to them. We observed this particularly in the Solidarity movement in Poland with its close ties to the Roman Catholic Church.

Frequently these Churches represent local populations in new forms of nationalism. The Polish Roman Catholic Church is the focal point for a national messianism in opposition to Russian domination and with strong anti-semitic overtones. Equally in the Baltic states the traditional Lutheran and Catholic Churches have been the focus for national identity. In the Ukraine and in various other former Soviet republics independence movements have been closely linked to the national church or to their roots in Islam. These religious backgrounds are deeply embedded in the culture of their people.

It was a moving experience to attend an early morning service one Saturday in an Orthodox church in Central Asia. About a thousand people stood for three hours in the crowded church as the solemn chanting of the liturgy gradually unfolded. Standing next to an old lady, I was humbled to think that she was probably born at about the time of the 1917 Communist Revolution. All the people around me had been brought up under intense atheistic propaganda and fierce discrimination against Christians. Despite those long years of opposition and persecution, they had stood firm. And their faith had vanquished the might of Marxism. There were no liturgy books, but many of those present joined in the chants, knowing them by heart. There had been no Sunday schools or religious education for the youth, but still they knew the words of the extremely lengthy liturgy. I watched a young woman earnestly praying on her own at the back of the church; after a while the tears began to roll down her cheeks as she poured out her prayers. As an evangelical Christian I may have some serious doubts about the theology of these churches, and I may long for a biblical renewal which would reduce the importance given to Mary, the saints and the icons. On the other hand I cannot but be impressed by the endurance and spirituality of these churches and by the fact that they are so firmly rooted in their local cultures. We dare not ignore their significance for the future witness of the Christian faith in this part of the world. Young people flow into these churches to join the elderly and often uneducated Christians who have survived the furnace of communist persecution.

Nevertheless the cutting edge of biblical evangelism remains in more evangelical circles. Baptists, Pentecostals and other denominations have grown considerably since the 1989 revolutions and Gorbachev's perestroika. As we have already observed, they are often serious and outwardly old-fashioned and legalistic, but through the years they have maintained a strongly Christ-centred faith and good biblical teaching.

In these days they gain much from the many western Christians who come in with teaching and literature. But the advantages of this fellowship include real dangers. One church in Romania has had foreign visitors preaching every Sunday for a year or more. With the present freedom of travel, these churches are often flooded with foreign visitors, all of whom bring financial gifts plus their own brands of Christian teaching – different attitudes to the charismatic renewal, various taboos of legalism, every shade of theology about the millennium, baptism and church order. Chaos and divisions easily ensue. Churches sometimes begin to waste their energies on internal wrangles imported from the West, rather than concentrating their united efforts on the great open doors for evangelism today. We need to discern between what is biblically essential and what is secondary to the central truths of Christ. How one wishes that Christians from the West would demonstrate more humility and wisdom in their approaches to mission in Eastern Europe! We need to be much more sensitive and submit to the wishes of national church leaders.

The flood of expatriate Christians over the years since 1989 has in some cases resulted in considerable disenchantment. In a recent visit to Eastern Europe, I noticed how often local Christians made disparaging remarks about Christian workers from the West. They commented frequently on the fact that very few of them bothered to learn the language adequately and that they hardly adjusted at all to local culture. Many of them apparently had little relationship with local churches, preferring to build their own kingdoms and try to establish their own ministries. Local Christians listened with astonished excitement when I told them of the policy of the mission with which we worked in Asia. The mission had established good language courses and all new missionaries studied the language and culture full-time for a minimum of one year and often for two years. This was followed by an ongoing course of language study for the following two or three years with regular exams to check on progress. If we are to relate in depth with people and communicate effectively we need good standards of language learning.

Conclusion

In the past decade the world scene has changed. The cold war with the former Soviet Union has subsided with the collapse of the Communist empire, the Russian economy in tatters and even the mighty Red Army in very considerable disarray.

It would be a singularly unwise person today who dared to look into their crystal ball and pontificate concerning the future of Eastern Europe. Even the mighty Germany since reunification presents us with great uncertainties. The radically different economic systems of the two parts of Germany have not proved easy to bring together and very real divisions remain even after so many years. East Germans still feel they are second-class citizens in the united Germany. West Germans look down their wealthy noses in their plush Mercedes as they overtake a ramshackle East German vehicle on the motorway.

In many of the former Communist countries the extremes of nationalism, right-wing dictatorships and resurgent left-wing communists lurk in the wings ready to break into the vacuum and take power. In many of these countries the Mafia have become immensely powerful, using the economic chaos and social upheavals for their own corrupt benefit.

In all these uncertainties the Czech Republic seems at present to offer unique hope. A burgeoning capitalist economy with very little accompanying poverty sounds a note of optimistic expectancy – but even here public sector strikes demonstrate a materialistic dissatisfaction.

In the Muslim states of the former Soviet Central Asia there are other clouds threatening the calm. A new wave of Muslim oppression or even direct persecution could fall on the church. Although new ex-Muslim fellowships of indigenous local people are emerging, the great majority of the church remains Russian and uses the Russian language. The intoxicating combination of Islam and nationalism hangs over the church like a Damocles sword.

The wide open doors for mission in Eastern Europe force the western church to ask various questions. Will the excitement of mission in these countries deflect our attention from work in other parts of the world, so that we send fewer workers and less money to those areas where we have traditionally served? Will our prayers be so concentrated on Eastern Europe that we neglect other places? We are also encountering the Orthodox Church in a new way and having to discover what they really believe and practise. Can we honestly work in relationship to the Orthodox Church without compromising our faith? Do the mission principles we have so painfully learned in Africa, Latin America and Asia apply to the more European countries of the ex-communist world? How does that influence our cooperation with local indigenous churches? Does it raise question marks concerning the way we pour in financial and other material aid?

In Western Europe we should also ask the question, 'Will Eastern Europe influence us or can it only be the reverse?' Some Russian and other east European Christians have begun to notice that because of their wealth western Christians can introduce their denominations, para-church movements and particular spiritual emphases into former communist societies, but the strong and dynamic churches of the East cannot share their life and teaching with us. Money speaks even in spiritual matters.

In introducing our capitalistic materialism we not only bring relief and developmental assistance into their situations of often extreme economic hardship and ecological disaster, but freedom and personal initiative come together with all our social and moral problems. Economic development, religious freedom, the Mafia and pornography belong together in one package. We should face the challenge and rethink our approach in order to present a new holistic faith in which mutual service and humility replace the search for self-satisfaction. In eastern Europe Marxist atheism has been severely questioned, while religion has sometimes been seen as having truth. Western Europe has much to learn from the tragic experiences of Eastern Europe. Can they help us to appreciate in a new way the need in our societies for an adequate ideology of truth? Will we learn the grave error of trusting secular materialism, atheism and even Marxism as the basis of life?

10

How on earth does God work?

In this small book we have done a whistle-stop trip around the world to see something of what God is doing in different areas. Inevitably our jet has over-flown some parts of the world where different readers would have preferred to stop and visit. Having lived in Bermuda for some years in my youth, I am very aware that no mention has been made of the Caribbean islands or the other small islands in the Atlantic Ocean. Likewise we have not discussed the multitude of island states in the Pacific. And within the continents and groups which we have noted there are doubtless many significant omissions. In one small book we cannot examine every race and people.

I can only plead guilty to these failures. In defence it has to be said that the aim of this book was not to give information in detail concerning every aspect of God's work in every part of the world. The closest approximations to such a mammoth work are the *World Christian Encyclopedia* by David Barrett[5] and the already mentioned *Operation World*.[2]

But we cannot conclude this book without discussing Australia and New Zealand. While geographically they are located on the fringe of Asia, culturally and racially they belong to the western world. They sometimes seek to identify themselves as Asian, but actually they really cannot be included in any survey of Asia. Because they do not fit neatly into any other major world grouping, they have been left for this final chapter.

Australia houses a growing population of Chinese and other Asians which prospers and multiplies. Chinese churches also flourish and represent a significant potential for mission to China and throughout East Asia.

Roman Catholics and Anglicans form by far the largest Christian churches. Strong conservative evangelical traditions govern some areas of the Anglican church, particularly in the Sydney diocese. This strong biblical base has given the church particular strength and has also preserved the evangelical character of the Australian Church Mission Society.

Both Australia and New Zealand have struggled with their consciences with regard to the original native populations of their islands. Aboriginal rights in Australia and the equivalent for the Maoris in New Zealand have raised questions of human rights both in Christian and in secular consciences. The churches have also had to come to terms with the fact that these aboriginal peoples have different cultures from the dominant white population. And yet traditionally the churches have not in the past adapted their forms of life, worship or communication to these minority populations. The churches also face the challenge of helping aboriginals to gain a new identity with a satisfying sense of value and worth. The lack of tribal dignity and identity has pushed many into degrading poverty and moral collapse. Today's churches are seeking to face up to this challenge.

As in many western countries, the main traditional churches have suffered considerable decline in membership over the past decades. Mission and evangelism have therefore come onto the front burner in church life and debate, but it is not proving easy to change churches from a primary emphasis on pastoral ministry to the needed new dynamic of mission. Some more evangelical and charismatic churches have stemmed the tide of decline; and Pentecostal and new churches have also seen growth. But the bulk of churches in Australia continue to lose ground.

In the past New Zealand was often considered a beautiful but remote backwater, but in more recent years it has jumped into the vanguard of modern life. This has also been reflected in church life. The pious but rather traditionalist outlook of the farming community has given way to the outgoing bustle of city life and modernity. Many church buildings have been modernized or new ones built. The charismatic renewal has added a dynamic vitality to many which has broken through more staid values in the church. Although it is still said that there are in New Zealand more sheep than people, the sheep now walk with a new bounce and vital initiative!

In this book we have sketched out the widespread growth of God's church in the various continents. As Christians, we rejoice in the fact that we have the privilege in Christ of belonging to this huge family. In every country all around the world we have brothers and sisters. In our days we have opportunities for travel which our grandparents could hardly envisage. This allows us to experience the reality of loving relationships with sisters and brothers of different races and backgrounds. In our own countries too the multiracial nature of modern societies opens the door for the same wide experience.

The rate of change is startling. If we look back a hundred years, the churches in most parts of Asia and Sub-Saharan Africa were either non-existent or still in their infancy. The Protestant movements in Latin America had hardly begun, while the traditional mixture of animistic tribal religion with a veneer of primitive Roman Catholicism dominated people's allegiance. Even in the great international mission conference in Edinburgh in 1910 there were almost no indigenous delegates from the Third World. This demonstrates the radically progressive character of such pioneer missionaries as Hudson Taylor in China who was already emphasizing the vital importance of indigenous Christian leadership in the second half of the nineteenth century. Henry Venn and other great Anglican leaders in the nineteenth century had the same vision for the churches in Africa. Rufus Anderson in America also advocated self-supporting, self-governing national churches.

In the 1960s many critics predicted that the end of colonialism would lead inevitably to the death of the Christian churches in previously colonial areas. Prediction can be a dangerous game! Political independence encouraged the churches to develop their own national leadership. Under their own leaders the churches began to multiply and in the last thirty years, millions of new Christians have flocked into the churches, particularly in Africa. As a result some mission 'experts' drew graphs of the growth of the church to demonstrate that by the end of the millennium Africa would be a Christian continent. Their predictions have proved sadly untrue.

This rapid expansion of the church since national independence has been seen also in some countries of Asia. In Latin America a more tolerant and open-hearted attitude by the Roman Catholic Church since the second Vatican Council has opened the door for the work of the Holy Spirit in the mushrooming growth of Pentecostal, Baptist and other Protestant churches.

The 1974 Lausanne Conference formed a watershed for the development of evangelical churches. Until then few Third World Christian leaders were well known outside their own countries. But at Lausanne new household names emerged, particularly from Latin America and Africa. From Lausanne too there developed an urgent call for theological and biblical training in every part of the world. As a result many new Bible schools and theological colleges came into being with ever-increasing standards both academically and practically. Today we salute the widespread achievements of these training establishments. Large numbers of men and women of high spiritual and academic calibre have been well-trained for leadership in local churches and in wider mission. Gradually too such colleges are beginning to develop culturally appropriate forms of training and syllabus rather than just copying western models. It remains true however that they desperately need good biblical commentaries, theological books and other Christian material which relates to their own religious, philosophical and cultural context.

No longer can western Christians look down their paternalistic noses as they relate to their brothers and sisters in other parts of the world. In fact today the boot may have slipped onto the other foot, for generally it is not the western churches which manifest vitality and growth. It is often within the Third World churches that the tension between academic theological training and practical spiritual dynamic is being resolved. Sadly in the western churches those who are sound in biblical and theological study sometimes stand apart from the vision of dynamic outgoing evangelism and mission. Likewise, those who experience the vitality of the Holy Spirit both in their personal lives and in their mission sometimes show scant regard for a careful and disciplined exegesis of the Bible and for theology. In European churches it is proving hard to change mentalities and restructure church life and worship to fulfil Christ's command to be 'fishers of men' rather than just keepers of aquariums. The West has much to learn from others in these days. But we rejoice in the working of God in his church both in the West and around the world.

As we have noted, 1989 marked the end of the rule of Communism in many lands. It has been remarkable since then to observe the victory of the often poor and uneducated church over the apparently powerful forces of atheism. Despite years of

propaganda and persecution which marginalized
the church, God's people have held on to their faith.
In the former Soviet Union church membership
nosedived in the first ten years or so of Communist
opposition, but since then the church has been able
to hold steady and then in more recent years to show
remarkable growth. Statistics are unreliable, but
some people estimate that at least ten per cent of the
entire population of the former Soviet Union attends
church on a Sunday. Most of these are of course in
the Russian Orthodox Church, although the Baptists, Pentecostals and newer churches also have
significant congregations. These newer churches
vary considerably from strongly charismatic to definitely anti-charismatic.

In China under Chairman Mao, Christians had to
go underground to a large extent. Many in the West
thought that Chinese Christianity had met its end. But
God remained on the throne of China and he has kept
his people wonderfully. At the time of the Marxist
revolution the church in China was relatively small
with only a million or two members. Considerable
power still lay in missionary hands, so that the church
sometimes appeared to be just a copy of western
models. Through the fires of fierce persecution and
fearful suffering the church has not only been puri-
fied, but millions of new believers have been added.
Of course such horrific persecution always leaves
intense problems in its wake, and western observers
should not be naive about the life of the church in
formerly Communist countries. Lack of teaching,
stubborn traditionalism, disunity and mutual suspicion all remain as a legacy from the rule of Commu-

nism. It would be wrong to idealize the church in China, but with deeply thankful hearts we recognize the work of the Holy Spirit in giving his people an almost incredible endurance against terrible odds.

While western Christians love to enthuse about the life and growth of churches overseas, it has become fashionable to contrast this with stagnation and lifelessness in Europe. The demise of colonialism led at first to a bullish optimism in newly independent countries, but in Europe it has introduced a deeply self-critical sense of inferiority. Liberal criticism and secular materialism have combined to empty those churches which have not kept up to date in their presentation of an assured Christian message. Large numbers of traditional church-goers have left the churches. The increasing pressures of hectic busy lives have pushed people away from involvement in the church. As a result, church statistics have drifted downwards for several decades, but towards the end of the 1980s this trend has begun to be reversed.

Many in the West have become somewhat disillusioned with the false promises of rationalistic science and education. Ever since the heady days of flower power and reaction in the late 1960s and early 1970s, a growing hunger for spirituality has been developing. What began with a few young reactionaries with long hair and torn jeans has swelled into a major current in our whole culture. The widespread influence of New Age and more recently the arrival of post-modernism onto the scene have led to a real interest in anything spiritual. Even the anti-Christian media have had to respond with articles and programmes discussing more overtly spiritual movements in the life of the church. As Christians we are presented therefore with a major opportunity to demonstrate and preach the living reality of the resurrected Christ. Religion and spirituality are back on the agenda.

Particularly the newer charismatic churches and likewise the more charismatic churches within the older denominations have grown in numbers and influence. Their dynamic, exuberant disco-style worship and optimistic confidence give a cutting edge to their faith in a God who is alive today. Other evangelicals may note the often rather careless use of Scripture, but people are attracted to more youthful forms and their emphasis on a God who not only works miracles but also speaks in prophecy directly to his people. Latterly they have underlined the spiritual battle against demonic powers. Of course there is a danger in every overemphasized fad or fashion, but this emphasis on 'spiritual warfare' relates closely to the current growth of occultism through a revival of paganism, the spread of eastern religions together with New Age movements and a multitude of other spirit-related practices like astrology, ouija boards or the Dungeons and Dragons game.

Although the charismatic churches make considerable gains around the world these days, we need a balanced analysis which takes note of the fact that they are by no means alone in seeing success. In the cities we find large non-charismatic churches which also flourish and grow. And in village after village, struggling little churches with tiny handfuls of church-goers have come to life during this past decade and have grown. Perhaps they only had ten or fifteen in their services ten years ago and now have increased to fifty. Such little churches will not hit the headlines, nor will they trumpet their successes in the media, but we are living through days of spiritual upturn. In my own village, for example, the local Anglican church struggled with a mere fifteen on a Sunday when we first moved in; now we enjoy a warm fellowship with about seventy or eighty adults on a Sunday. During the 1980s many of the village churches in our area experienced growth with a change to more biblical and evangelical ministries. The Lord is at work in Europe too!

Bible Translation

Since the Second World War God has given Christians a determined desire to get the Bible translated into all the many languages in every part of the world. The professional expertise of Wycliffe Bible Translators together with the International Bible Society has led the way. Wycliffe have sent large numbers of their members into many tribal groups to reduce their languages to writing, teach people to read and also translate God's word. Their linguistic expertise has been passed on to missionaries in many other missionary societies so that this vital work may be achieved more effectively and speedily. In some countries, national translation societies have been established through the work of Wycliffe Bible Translators so that local people can be trained to do the work of translation without being subject to foreign bodies.

In many situations the existing Bible translations in national languages were made a long time ago and have become outdated. My wife and I remember the excitement and hunger when a revised New Testament in our local language in Indonesia came into print. At first we had to ration it, only allowing two copies into each village church until larger stocks became available. As we know from European church history, God's Holy Spirit changes lives and whole societies when the Bible is widely read by people in their own language. We also know how vital it has been in English to have more modern translations which ordinary people can read easily.

When the Bible is translated into a local language, it makes people aware that the Christian gospel belongs to them and relates to them as a people. This may be particularly true in a Muslim context, for the Qur'an is rarely translated into the languages of minority peoples. They will have to use Arabic and perhaps some majority trade language for all religious purposes. In this way God can appear distant and unrelated to them. The translation of the New Testament into their language can then demonstrate the reality that the Christian faith identifies with them and their culture.

We should, however, note a possible danger in some Bible translation work. In many parts of Africa the spectre of tribalism haunts the nation. In contrast to such tribal divisions, the church may well have developed along inter-tribal lines with its worship and teaching in a common trade language. The translation of the Bible into each tribal language may just encourage the church to divide along tribal lines. So the witness of the gospel in a divided society may be impaired.

Nevertheless we cannot forget the immense privilege of being able to read God's word in our own language. What a privilege!

Every year we see a flow of Bible translations coming into print. One by one the thousands of different languages have God's word translated into them. On a recent visit to Central Asia it was exciting to see the new edition of the Bible in the national language of that country. It had been printed in the style of the Muslim Qur'an as the local culture has a Muslim background. The authorities had noted the excellence of its style and the beauty of its language, so they had ordered thousands of copies for school libraries. It will surely have a marked influence on that whole society as it evolves in the coming days.

There are however many languages which still do not have the Bible. Well trained workers are needed for this significant task. But it is exciting to note the tremendous progress which has been made in recent years.

Training

The life and growth of the church under the Holy Spirit depends largely on the development of well trained leaders with spiritual vitality. Training for church leadership stands at the head of any list of mission priorities. We have already observed the spread of Bible schools and theological colleges in the Third World since the 1974 Lausanne Conference.

Increasingly evangelicals have begun to take biblical and theological studies much more seriously, so that they now play a major part in giving the lectures and writing the books which form the thinking of the next generation of church leaders – and then through them their ordinary church members.

But generally speaking, full-time theological colleges and Bible schools can only train a relatively small number of top leaders. Expanding churches need more than this. Latin America has seen the development of many 'night Bible institutes' in which people study after their day's work. Latin America also pioneered theological education by extension, a system in which lecturers travel out to groups of students in their home areas rather than students gathering in the centralized Bible school. In this way groups of Christians can meet in their housing area or village each week to discuss the previous week's private study, gain further input from the lecturer and also enjoy the fellowship and interaction of the group. Theological education by extension has widened out from its original Latin American base, being used now in every continent. It has the potential of being able to train Christian leaders at every level in much larger numbers.

More and more churches in Europe and elsewhere have become aware of the vital significance of training Christians biblically and practically for evangelism and service. Some local churches have started one year programmes of teaching and training. Sometimes groups of churches from the same denomination or in the same locality have clubbed together to run such training programmes. Of course these local initiatives may lack the theological or mission expertise of a full-time establishment, but they play a significant role in training Christians for service locally.

It is encouraging to see the adventurous spirit with which Christians are experimenting with new forms of training for Christian leadership and service. And the theological colleges, Bible schools and mission training establishments continue their essential role in training the pastors and missionaries of the future. Other part-time or short-term initiatives cannot compete with their professional expertise. The growth of evangelical scholarship in biblical, theological and missiological subjects bodes well for the future of God's church.

Social awareness

In the past evangelicals were often accused of being interested only in people's souls with little concern for their bodies or for society. A more careful reading of missionary records shows considerable emphasis on social ministries and even political involvement for the sake of those suffering discrimination. On the other hand, evangelical magazines and other writings have sometimes played down social and political concerns because they knew their constituencies' dislike of a theologically liberal 'social gospel'.

Today evangelical Christians have jumped on the bandwagon of concern for the oppressed. We have become deeply aware of the biblical emphasis on justice and God's love for the poor. Likewise evangelicals take a lead in ecological debate and action on behalf of the environment. We play our part in trying to preserve endangered animal species, prevent deforestation and encourage ecologically sustainable development.

Indeed there is sometimes a danger that we can lose sight of our traditional belief in personal sin and in reconciliation with God through the atoning death of Jesus Christ on the cross. Holistic Christian faith must include both the socio-political dimension and also the more directly spiritual. But no one today can justifiably accuse evangelical Christians generally of being unthinking right-wing traditionalists. It is encouraging to notice a passionate concern which has led to pioneering work for drug addicts, AIDS sufferers, the homeless and other suffering or marginalized people. The plight of street children has moved the hearts of evangelicals in more recent years, and practical action has ensued. Evangelical Christians play a significant part today in pressure groups working for greater justice. Ecological concern for the flora and fauna of our threatened world is leading to new forms of Christian mission where the preaching of Jesus Christ and church planting go hand in hand with ornithology and other practical ecological ministries. Of course, more still could be done and there are still many who lack such concern, but God's Holy Spirit is moving his people to love their needy neighbours.

Sadly the tension between God-centred spiritual ministries and more neighbour-centred social concerns remains. Much thought has gone into mission theories which stress the inseparable nature of these two emphases. It is often pointed out that social ministries are not just tin-openers to prepare the way for evangelism, but are in themselves an essential part of Christian mission. Yet those who emphasize this truth sometimes have less sympathy for fellow Christians who concentrate on purely evangelistic mission.

While it is often noted that social ministry does frequently lead to more effective and credible evangelism, few seem to believe that a right relationship with God might bring social and even political benefits. This is understandable, for history presents us with too many cases where committed Christians have failed totally to stand for the rights of the oppressed. Likewise we see too many committed Christians who are deeply involved in loving work for marginalized minorities and even in political action for the sake of justice, but who seem to ignore people's need for evangelism and eternal life. We need therefore to be reminded again and again that God is concerned both for evangelism and social action.

In fact social change does often follow in the wake of evangelism and the growth of the church. In our area of Indonesia it was not acceptable for men to do hard muscular work – in the old days men did the fighting, but in modern times they just sat around gossiping, drinking tea and gambling. But as the message of Christ permeated society, men began to join their wives in the fields. This not only changed the local economy for the better, but also brought a greater sense of oneness into marriage relationships. In the fertile Kathmandu valley in Nepal, the animistic spirits in the local Hindu religion have forbidden people from using any machinery in agriculture or transport in the valley. This has seriously hindered agricultural productivity. If the people of Nepal became Christians, it would lead also to more food through better agriculture.

In our day God is at work, moving Christians to rethink the relationship of the gospel to political, ecological and social issues, and then motivating us to action.

One God – many ways of working

Open-minded readers of this book may have observed how God works through different agencies in the various parts of the world. In Latin America the Pentecostals have been the most significant instrument of the Holy Spirit, while in Korea and Indonesia the massive growth of the church has come largely through the Reformed churches. In West Africa the churches planted by interdenominational missions play important roles in the overall life of the church of God, while in East Africa the mainline Anglicans and Lutherans host the revival work of the Holy Spirit. In Malaysia and Singapore the charismatic renewal has brought new life to the Methodists and Anglicans with considerable church growth as a result. In Europe too the charismatic movement has played a highly significant part in the whole development of church life and its churches often spearhead church growth in various of our countries. Thus far the growth of charismatic churches has been largely concentrated in big towns and cities, but there are already some signs that this may overflow into villages and rural areas too.

Of course each of the above generalizations is too simplistic. In Latin America many other churches besides the Pentecostals show considerable growth. In West Africa the mainline denominations cannot be ignored, while in East Africa the Africa Inland Church was founded by a non-denominational mission and has become one of the largest churches of that area. In no part of the world can God be pigeonholed to such a degree that he can only work in one particular type of church.

It is important to note that our God is bigger than just our favourite form of Christianity. Some Christian literature dismisses the charismatic renewal as a maverick and temporary phenomenon of no ultimate significance. This is just not true to the facts. In many parts of the world it is the charismatic and Pentecostal churches which flourish more than any others. But some other Christian literature is equally one-sided in its emphasis that God only works significantly through charismatic churches. The facts of our contemporary world deny this equally. Not only are most of the huge Reformed churches of Korea and Indonesia not charismatic, but even in Latin America many anti-charismatic churches catch our attention with their vitality and growth. In the mushrooming 'House Churches' of China there is great diversity, but most are not charismatic in their emphasis.

When one travels to other countries, denominational flexibility and the ability to appreciate other expressions of the Christian faith become particularly important. Denominations which are centre-stage in one country may be quite peripheral in another; Christian movements which have a good name in one area may have a different history elsewhere and thus a different reputation.

Our responsibility

John Wesley affirmed that Christians should bend their backs to assist the work of the Holy Spirit. We have therefore to ask what the Holy Spirit is actually doing in the world today. Through the chapters of this book we have observed a little of God's activities in the various continents and among different peoples. Now our task is to work together with God in his mission. This will be achieved as we come to the Lord in prayer for the world and for his guidance as to what part he wants us to play.

As we have talked about different areas of the world we have noted not only the positive elements of what God has been doing, but also some of the negatives of what still remains to be done. We have felt the strengths of various churches around the world, but we have also grieved at some of the weaknesses. Such an awareness of the tremendous needs in our world can overwhelm us with a sense of our fearful inadequacy. What can little people like us do in the face of such pressures? But the knowledge of the world's and the church's needs can also stimulate us to a new sense of responsibility. God has not called us to become his disciples merely for our self-satisfaction and salvation, but also in order to serve his church and the world. As we gain information about what God is doing in the world, our response whispers to God: 'Lord, what do you want me to do? I am ready to do anything anywhere for you.' And God's authority and enabling will work through our weakness – we can trust him.

The New Testament states firmly, 'You are not your own; you were bought with a price' and then commands in consequence 'So glorify God in your body' (1 Cor. 6:19,20). In Jesus Christ God has paid an incalculable price for our salvation and has redeemed us for himself and for his service. The great purpose of our life now is to glorify God. It should sadden us to observe how his name is dragged in the mud, blasphemed, misunderstood or ignored. We long that people everywhere should honour him and love him as is his due. To this end we dedicate our lives.

Notes

1 Sinclair, M., *Ripening Harvest, Gathering Storm* (Tunbridge Wells: Monarch, 1988)
2 Johnstone, P., *Operation World* (Carlisle: Send the Light, 1986)
3 Gaukroger, S., *Why Bother with Mission?* (London: Evangelical Missionary Alliance, 1996)
4 For further reading on the subject, see Goldsmith, M., *What About Other Faiths?* (London: Hodder & Stoughton, 1989)
5 Barrett, D., *World Christian Encyclopaedia* (Oxford: Oxford University Press, 1982)